FIRST YOU THEN HIM

A FORMER TRAINWRECK'S GUIDE TO BECOMING THEN FINDING A HEALTHY PARTNER

NINYA

NINYA

PRAISE FOR FIRST YOU THEN HIM

You picked up this book because part of you **knows** this is how it is supposed to work.

First You Then Him: A Former Trainwreck's Guide to Becoming then Finding a Healthy Partner is a title that really does say it all.

There are hundreds of self-help books on the market that want to tell you *who to be* in order to find the "perfect mate." Ninya, on the other hand, wants to help you learn and grow in WHO YOU ARE.

- How can you be in a healthy relationship with others if you aren't in a healthy relationship *with yourself*?
- How can you attract and keep a good partner if you don't know *how to be a* good partner?
- How can you find a positive partner if you don't know *what you want or need* in a partner?

These are just some of the down-to-earth questions Ninya tackles with humor, experience, and (most importantly) detailed steps to begin finding answers that work for you.

Unlike a stuffy classroom lecture or someone's Ph.D. research on self-esteem as it relates to relationship quality, Ninya presents a life lived. She shares mistakes and heartaches we can relate to. She offers insight learned in the school of hard knocks and then breaks it all down into a starting point for readers to gain insights into their own patterns, needs, directions for growth.

Some may need every chapter in this book; others may feel only a few chapters resonate with them right now. Parents, partners, and friends may also find this book useful with helping the people they love. Regardless of who you are or where you are in your journey, there is something here for you. I just wish it had been published twenty years ago!

To all the little girls who grew up listening to fairy tales with hearts in their eyes only to find out they were lies: Your true love is already here. She is you.

XOXO Ninya

FIRST YOU

WHAT DO I KNOW?

This book is called First You, Then Him for a reason. I had it backward in thinking that finding the right relationship was the key to my happiness. It took me a really long, and I mean a *really, really* long time to acknowledge and fix my own problems. Finally, I understood that I was the common denominator that I brought into every relationship. It took another four painful years to figure out this one truth. If you aren't healthy, then it is only a matter of time before even the best relationship crumbles.

I would lament over pitchers and pitchers of margaritas with girlfriends that my picker was broken, instead of looking at myself first. The work of fixing myself was not fun, or sexy, and not a priority for me. After being so miserable in the wrong marriage, I was on a quest to make my life exciting again, pronto, and I was so sure that 100% of the answer was choosing the right guy. I started new relationship after new relationship, on a quest for happiness that crashed and burned every time. It got frustrating. I wasted so much time. Yet, I kept repeating this vicious cycle, thinking, eventually, I would get it right when I found the right guy. Wrong!

My biggest pet peeve is wasting time. Considering I languished sixteen years in the wrong marriage, you would say (correctly) that the evidence doesn't support this theory. But, in reality, it was one of those situations where I finally woke up and then looked in the mirror and said, *Damn, Girl! You're almost all used up! You wasted your skinny, pretty years on the wrong guy. Now you must immediately hunt down the right one, bag him and tag him, and then get married as quickly as possible to right this wrong. You need to prove to yourself and everyone else that you aren't the complete train wreck you believe yourself to be.*

I should have started with me. I can see that clearly now. Hindsight is 20/20, after all, but at the time, I was so focused on proving I could have a healthy relationship if I just worked hard enough at it.

What the heck do I know? That's a very good question to ask. Whenever you pick up a book that is supposed to make your life better in some way or improve your current state, you need to assess if this person is worth listening to. I have been through it. If you want a glimpse into that, my Scotland memoir is ready and waiting for you to read. The last decade of my life, from mid-thirties to mid-forties, has been especially punishing… er, I mean, filled with wisdom and hard lessons. After finally finding the right guy at nearly 45, I decided to undertake the task of helping my younger sisters navigate their way through the shitshow of finding yourself, modern dating, and relationships. I love who I have become now through this process. Jokingly with girlfriends, I have said more than once, "Man, I wish I could go back to my twenties knowing what I know now! If only to slap the shit out of myself, for all the mistakes I made." Dear lawd, there were *so* many! Those lessons were hard-won victories. Confucius say: "With wrinkles and age spots come great understanding."

This book is the book I wish I had read when I was twenty. If I'd had a resource like this, I would have saved myself so much pain and agony, so many years of frustration and anxiety. Not to mention, tens of thousands of dollars in therapy, divorce lawyers, and other financial debacles, but I didn't and I suffered. I want to give people a blueprint to fixing themselves and then finding a healthy partner because I truly believe that ninety percent of your happiness, or your pain, in this life comes from the person you choose to partner with. If you choose well, life becomes infinitely easier, as two are able to carry the burden of raising a family and all the hard things that inevitably come during the day to day living of a lifetime together. If you make a bad choice, then you will likely pay the price for at least decades, maybe forever, stuck with a person who actively works against you instead of as a teammate. That life becomes a bitter pill to swallow and sets you up for a lifetime of struggle.

My low self-worth and flawed picker led me down many a shifty side alley, from the boy who peed on my clothing on the floor after one night of partying (talk about a whole new urine-soaked walk of shame!) to the guy who impregnated someone else while I was all in on the relationship and blissfully unaware. I have dated all the bad apples, and now I know one when I see it.

So, this is me, holding out a hand to you, offering to pull you off the struggle bus. Let my wasted decades light your way. Learn the lessons I had to learn without the pain of actually going through them. If this book resonates, send it to a young woman you love. You will give them the tools to design a better life. I wish I knew what is contained here when I was twenty years old. Oh, how things would have been different.

P.S. I SAY 'HIM' but these principles are almost always universal, no matter who you love.

HOW TO USE THIS BOOK

More than anything, I hope this book serves as a catalyst for change in your life. I hope, as you read through the pages, you are forced to examine your life more closely. That you take a really deep dive into where you are right now and plot a plan for better. It's one thing to tell you my sad stories and point out the places where I fell down the well, but it's another entirely for you to turn the focus of these lessons inward.

Don't get overwhelmed by where you are right now. Growth is constant. The person I was in my twenties and the person I am now are so vastly different from each other because of the personal growth I have experienced. No matter where you find yourself right now, single or partnered, introvert or social butterfly, you will find something here to inspire your own transformation. There is so much damage and brokenness out there that, even if you are the rare breed that grew up surrounded by healthy relationships, chances are there are lessons here that will help you understand your friends or partners who weren't so lucky. Self-examination and taking the time to heal yourself is never wasted time.

One tool I have used my entire adult life is journaling. It has been a north star for me and a glimpse into my own heart when things seem convoluted and hard to process. It also became a place to document the things that have happened so I could refer to them later. Traumatic events have a way of changing your brain and rewriting your memories. It goes into self-preservation mode and hides painful events by compartmentalizing, so resources are freed up for basic things like breathing and working. My brain is so good at tucking the bad stuff away into the deepest corners of my mind that I find myself having to read over past journal entries to remember. My entries bring it back in the *Oh yeah, I remember that now. Man, I have been through some serious shit. Cue up "Eye of the Tiger" way.*

I encourage you to start the practice of journaling. Just a few pages written every day can have a profound impact on your life if you let it. I know journaling isn't sexy and seems like work. You might be rolling your eyes and smacking your hand against your head at the very thought of putting the craziness in your mind on paper. You might think journaling is a stupid waste of time, or my handwriting sucks, or I am not a writer.

You don't have to physically sit down with your journal and a cuppa tea with Yanni in the background while you diffuse lavender essential oils into your space. You can. But you can also choose to open a word doc and bash the keyboard. The point is, you need to set aside some time to focus on your life and the lessons within the pages of this book. By writing the words, whether longhand or on a computer, there will be breakthroughs that you never saw coming. You will find a clarity that you have never known. It will be a place to put your fears to get them out of your own head, so you can look at them from a distance and with detachment.

This will make your decisions easier. It will relieve your stress, and it will give your friends a break if you are the type of person who loves to tell a sob story. Journaling is the cheapest therapy available. During critical times of my own life, instead of lying in bed and letting the anxiety machine crank up endlessly, I have gotten out of bed and given myself the gift of a brain dump. I got all the negativity out of my head so I could be a normal person again.

You don't have to journal. You don't. You can read the book, think about the concepts, and likely make some real changes without putting a pen to paper, ever. But I believe you are cheating yourself. You are taking a shortcut, and I know from years of experience that taking the shortcuts don't get you to the place you want to be. Working toward growth and change takes a disciplined effort, and one of the tools that will help you immensely is journaling. I know it works, and that is why I encourage it.

Sometimes, when I am working through a very difficult decision, I don't know what I think until I journal about it. It is the process of collecting all those stray thoughts and finding them a home so you can travel through your day lighter and undistracted. It will give you clarity and focus like nothing else.

You bought the book. You are committed to reading it. So, do yourself the favor and go all in. Go all in on your self-transformation. Spend at least fifteen to thirty minutes journaling on the takeaway questions at the end of each chapter. Don't take the easy route. Dig deep. Do the things you don't want to do, and power through to the other side. It's a beautiful place to be, and I am waiting over there for you to break through with fresh lemonade and warm chocolate chip cookies.

Do the work. There are no shortcuts.

WHO ARE YOU?

When you were born, you innately knew. Inside your DNA was the clear authentic truth of your being. You simply were you. Then began the bulk of the work of childhood, to control and shape you into what society wanted you to be, to force you into submission, to become a cog in the collective machine of the world. You allowed your parents and caregivers to rub their fears onto you and show you the path of least anxiety all in the name of love. They spoke of college educations and becoming lawyers and doctors and accountants, anything that would certainly secure your future but not your happiness. You listened to them and convinced yourself to be practical, probably calming the worries of your parents by fitting into the box of who they wanted you to be. But this thinking was fundamentally flawed. You were forced into that box, but eventually, you felt trapped, desperate to claw your way out for fresh air. You either stayed trapped and died a little every day, or you plotted an escape, freeing yourself from your loving captors who were loving you to death.

For years, I was trapped. I spent so much time ignoring who I truly was in order to keep the business going, in order to feed my family, in order to fill the cupboards and my 401k. After about two decades of ignoring and stuffing my true self, the inevitable identity crisis cued up. I began to value happiness over money, and the disconnect led me to undertake my own journey that brought me closer to my true self. It is a journey that has no end. Every day brings fresh lessons or repeats of the ones I wasn't open to receiving the first time around.

This journey is a scary one because it usually unfolds with a dramatic plot twist that will make your family shudder in terror. The journey for me began when I finally acknowledged my true vocation. I am a writer. I discovered this late in life after denying myself for twenty years. Even though I have written in journals almost daily since I was eleven, I never put the two together. Even though I have started three novels, I let the fears that I could never be published and actually make money as an author stop my progress, but not anymore. I *am* a writer. By clearly defining who I am, I am putting my mind into a headspace that is decisive and smaller. I am limiting what my future prospects look like, which brings me into deeper alignment with them. It is burning the boats, knowing that I will find a way to survive in this space, somehow, some way.

When you finally commit to something, there is a shift in the universe and a huge difference in what it sends you in terms of opportunities and people. The clarity is so helpful because, when you are a jack of all trades to the universe, it supports you in becoming the master of none.

I am scared to death. This is totally normal. I am getting up in faith, writing for hours nearly every day, and proving to God that I am truly a writer. Since a writer writes, I am dutifully sitting down at my computer every day and writing. Even though I have no idea how I will finish this, how I will edit it, or how I will sell it. Even though the voices have started screaming in my head that I have no idea what I am doing, that I am an imposter, a fake, and a fraud. These are all questions I will work through down the road. The important thing now is that I am taking action toward what I want. I am allowing the flow toward who I truly am to pull me in its current. Instead of fighting it and choking on fear and struggling to breathe, completely exhausted, I am naturally allowing the work to flow through me without judging how good it is. I get up, I make my coffee, and I write. It is as simple as that.

Years ago, it became obvious I needed a clean break from my previous income source. The universe agreed with me and sent my ex-husband to lay me off from a business I helped him found. "I just can't do this anymore," he said. "You're killing me." I remember that moment so clearly. We stood out on my crappy apartment's third-floor balcony so he could chain smoke while he delivered the news. When the words left his lips, we both knew instinctively they were true, but it thrust me out of the nest before I was ready to fly. I was taking tentative steps toward uncovering who I was and who I wanted to be, but I was too comfortable knowing that there was no real danger of trying something when I had the business to fall back on.

After our long, messy divorce, working with him in any capacity was bad for me. In order to heal completely and move in the direction I wanted to go, I had to free myself from my past and my reliance on him. The security of that income went up in smoke like the cigarettes he smoked that day on my patio. He left and then fear set in, screaming in my ear. The fear will tell you terrible things that are not true. *You will never succeed. You are only a back-*

ground player. Look at all your previous failures. You can't do this.

I am learning to tell that voice to STFU by punishing the keys on my computer. I am capable, my work has value, and I will be successful. I will contribute to the world and use my gifts to the greatest service I can, and I will not let fear force me to play small anymore. When I was in Scotland, I met a sweet older gentleman at the pub named Duncan. We talked about life a bit, and he talked about a cancer diagnosis that put his life in perspective.

He asked, "What do you do?" I told him I was a writer, even though I had not officially published anything but blog posts. He looked me dead in the eyes and said, "It is time for you to be out there. You have been in the background far too long. Trust the message you have to say and put yourself out there." Even thousands of miles away from home, the universe sent me a love note, a clue that said, *Hey girl! You're on the right track.*

For far too long, I settled and toiled for years, taking care of my family and working jobs that didn't fulfill my purpose. I did accounting, sold insurance, did data entry, and social media marketing. All were career paths that didn't energize me or tap into my true gifts. They were sensible and good enough, but none of them lit me up like writing did.

I kind of have this visual that, in heaven, right before we are born, we are all babies sitting and waiting on the puffy clouds. One by one, we get our anointing, where God places his hand on our forehead and whispers, "You're a football player. You're an artist. You're an activist. You're a scientist." He bestows one bright shining quality on each of us that is the clearest expression of who you are and what you have been sent here to do.

Sometimes you are lucky and, as children, you can see and begin to develop this quality. Sometimes you are stuck in fear and can't acknowledge it quite yet. But, over time, the yearning to express this becomes deafening, drowning out everything else until it is all you can hear, and you are forced to act. The work becomes about stripping away everything you are *not* until you truly discover who you *are* in the simplest, most minimal sense.

You strip away layers of fear and anxiety and distrust. You let the light in to supercharge your soul gift—it's solar since, in my mind, God was the OG environmentalist—and you start to shine. There are so many people merely existing with darkness inside. They haven't done the work or are afraid to do the work to turn their lights on. I believe it is my duty to encourage others to do this, and that is what drives me at two a.m. when the insomnia is off the charts to write these words.

The world needs more people that are glowing from their own internal light. We need more fearless soul-renovating warriors whose battle cry is "I AM…" Who *you* are is enough. Who *you* are is important. Who *you* are will give your life meaning in the most beautiful way. It will bring clarity and peace to you in a way that nothing else will. Find your light and turn that baby on. Let it burn brightly in the truth and acceptance of who you are. If you have ever been to a concert or a vigil or a midnight mass on Christmas, and you have been part of a candlelight service, you know the power of standing together in a crowd with your fire glowing. You know how breathtakingly beautiful that is to experience. I think you can have that every day if you are simply brave enough to light it.

The Big Takeaway Question: Who are you?

Who are you at your core without all the other people in your life making your decisions for you? If you don't know where to start, the clues are in your childhood. What did you love to do for hours on end? What activities made you lose track of time? What are you naturally good at? What have people told you that you excel at without even trying? What makes your heart race?

There are professional ice cream testers—it's a legit career—so don't judge anything that feels authentic for you.

FEAR OF AUTHENTICITY

When you were a kid, it was easy to be authentic. You just were who you were. You didn't overthink it. You didn't consider what other people would think of you, you just did you. Then, around the time you started going to school, you learned to perform. You started to learn that people wouldn't like you if you didn't do the things they wanted you to do. So, you started to hide who you were, little by little, day by day, year by year. The very essence of you eroded under the weight of fitting in and meeting the expectations of others.

To satisfy your need to belong, you found yourself making concessions, some of them big and some of them small that, over time, compounded into something huge. Like when a pilot makes a one-degree adjustment to the controls and you end up in Newark instead of Boca Raton. You are so far away from who you truly are that it feels foreign. You feel disconnected at your core and struggle to find your way back.

Self-love's cornerstone is authenticity. It is being able to look at yourself in the mirror as you truly are and still love what you see. If you don't love yourself or aren't being authentic, then the disconnect hurts. It is the pebble in the shoe that is the seed of many midlife crises.

The best way back to yourself is to make little changes and shifts that align with who you are. As you change, you will scare others who are running around smearing their worries all over you. "What? You want to leave your job and homeschool? You don't even know the Pythagorean theorem!" Their worries and fears are based on their own insecurities. Even well-meaning people, like your parents, think it is their job to protect you and often do so by cranking up the worry machine. You must continue your work of uncovering yourself, despite the fact this will scare them even more. Some people will fall away, unable to join you on this journey, and you must let them go. Not everyone you meet or bring into your life is going to be there for the long haul. They might be a catalyst for a particular time and then may disappear, and that is okay. New people will show up in their place that fit where you are going if you are open to letting them in.

Each change you make will draw you a little closer to who you are. You must peel back the layers and strip away all the masks you were forced to wear to fit in. If it has been a long time, it will feel more like an archeological dig, with your pickaxe and broom, uncovering who you were at your core, before you buried it under the weight of everyone else's expectations, needs, and wants.

I found that, even though in theory it is quite simple, it is some of the hardest work today because of all the fear. In my early forties, I was at a crossroads professionally. I had transitioned out of the business I built with my ex-husband. I tried and failed at a few smaller projects on my own, floundering a bit, and the fear was screaming in my ears. Some days, it was the only thing I heard.

I adore Brené Brown. If I met her in real life, I would probably pee on the floor a little out of excitement, like the dachshund I used to have. I discovered her books and devoured them in days, and it truly opened my eyes to how far I was away from the authentic life I wanted to live. I was desperate to find the truth of who I was and to start living from that place authentically. I figured that I probably had about another forty years to live if I was lucky and took care of myself, and so I was looking for ways to make the back forty the most successful of my life. By that time, the word success for me was very different than it was in my twenties. Success wasn't just money and possessions. It was fulfillment and alignment and living the way I wanted to live and how I wanted to live and where I wanted to live. Yes, I needed money to do all these things, because money is a tool. Not the only tool, but a really important one because of its transformative nature.

So, how could I align who I am with my need to be self-sufficient and support myself and my kids? I have always been a writer, for as long as I can remember, but I never called myself one by name until just recently. I have journaled and written poems and short stories. When I was a little girl, I would sit on my bed for hours with my sister, and we would write stories. In my late twenties, I started a writing club with my sister and a new friend and started a novel I never finished. All of these were clues to my authentic self, but society had covered me in its fears of failure and not being good enough for so long, even I couldn't see who I was or what I was put here to do.

How do you know if you are taking the right steps toward authenticity? They feel good. They feel natural. Things begin to flow. Opportunities and people start coming into your life to support the authentic you. I started small, with a blog, and called it my midlife crisis. About seven people read it, but I didn't care. I wrote anyway. I started writing a new book. I connected with an author in my neighborhood, and we hit it off right away. The guy I was dating said, "You should write a book." Hearing those words spoken out loud gave me permission to run harder toward my dream. I set aside time to write every day. I set word count goals and joined a Facebook group to learn about self-publishing. I made friends with authors, real people who were out there doing what I felt I was born to do.

All of these small steps started to peel away the layers of gunk, and the light crept in to illuminate the next steps I should take. At first, I was just journaling to clear my mind after years of traumatic experiences. Last year, I wrote a blog post where I declared my intention to the world as my way of burning the boats. I am a writer. Writers write. I do that, so I am a writer. End of story. This year, I published a real book, with an ISBN number and everything, so now I am a published author. End of story. Each step taken toward this dream feels right and good. It is me, with tears in my eyes, saying to myself, "Hey, I remember you. It's *so* good to see you again. I have missed you so much."

Another dream is to have a book on the New York Times Bestsellers list because my mom lived and died by that list. "Have you read blah blah blah? It's a New York Times Bestseller!" I wake up every day and envision a book cover with my name and those words, and someday that will be a reality. When people ask me what I do, I tell them I am a writer. It's my way of owning who I am and of claiming my space in this world. It's me telling the universe that I finally know what I am. I am a writer, so send me what I need to be legit. Please and thank you.

With my relationships, authenticity is about truth. It's about listening to my heart and approaching whatever is happening in the relationship from a real place. It's taking the time to own myself and what is good for me. It's setting and maintaining standards that don't undermine me or set me up to do something I do not want to do. It is being mature enough to have the hard conversations when things don't go well or cross into a place that isn't good for me.

Relationships teach you so many things you need to know about your authentic self. They give you a lab to conduct experiments in real-time. You can either combine two elements and cause an explosion, or you can put your goggles on, adjust the burner, and keep everything in the tube. You have the choice every single day. You get to test out how to respond to people when they hurt you, how your own insecurities can get in the way of something that is good. You discover the intensity and insanity of love and how transforming it can be when you show up authentically and are accepted fully. They can also be painful punishers if you aren't being truthful with yourself and the ones you love. You can take a back seat or stuff your emotions, and then you know you are off course because it feels bad. You know in your gut that something isn't right.

This is why discovering who you are and what you need is so critical. If you know who you are and what you need, the right relationship is easy. Because, at your core, you know you are enough on your own. Your partner doesn't have to do or be anything for you because you are enough already. Being with a person that adds to your already full life is incredible. Being with someone because you need them to fill your emptiness is torture, for both of you.

Look for examples of people living authentically all around you. They are few but so inspiring. I love Alyssa Edwards, a drag queen from Texas. She is the very definition of authenticity for me—lit up and in love with life, doing work she loves, unafraid to step totally into herself. That's amazing, and that is where I aspire to be. I challenge you to uncover and step out unabashedly into your own truth so you can claim your rightful place in this world. The world needs you to be who you are, to live at your highest authentic self, and to encourage others to do the same.

The Big Takeaway Questions: What concessions have I made in order to belong? What steps can I take to align with my true self?

Adapt the one step closer philosophy. Pick one small thing you can do every day that will move you closer to the authentic you. The step should feel good. That is how you know it is right. Note: I did not say the step would be easy. Sometimes they are, but more often, it takes work and focused effort to step into a more authentic place in your heart and your life.

List three examples of people living authentically. Who inspires you to be true to yourself?

WHERE'S THE SELF LOVE, SISTA?

At nearly forty-three, it dawned on me, out of the blue on a random Sunday morning, that I did not love myself. Self-love conjures up endless masturbation jokes for me because my sense of humor is in line with a twelve-year-old boy, and so I pretty much avoided the topic for most of my life. That day, the sun shined bright on this dark and dusty corner of my self-awareness attic, and I said out loud, "I don't love myself." At the time, it was an epiphany. I knew it was true because it resonated deeply.

To say those words aloud felt stupid and whiny, but obviously, my actions proved it to be true. The punishing back to back relationships with the wrong people and keeping them in my life entirely too long. Pushing past my own wants to sacrifice for others. And then there was the negative self-talk, the body shaming, and cycles of binge eating and hating. The psoriasis flare-ups that made me angry and itchy and ashamed of the plaques running down the back of my neck and forehead.

The choices I was making reflected the deep self-hatred I

felt. Instead of choosing a relationship with a man who loved me to my core and wanted to truly build a life with me, I chose a man who pursued me and then made me live on edge with his anxiety rubbing against mine so hard a fire always erupted. People took things from me, and what was left over, I gave away until I was completely depleted and a shell of what I had been. I gave until it hurt, trying to ease the guilt about my broken marriage and how it impacted my children. The self-loathing was automatic and intense. My internal dialogue, if it was typed up and read aloud, would shock most people. On the outside, I was smiling and joking, but on the inside, I was punishing myself for the mistakes that I had made. It was an endless loop of insults that filled the quiet in my mind, a repeat reel that cued up the moment my eyes opened in the morning and didn't quit until I fell asleep that night.

One day, it occurred to me that I would NEVER speak to a friend the way I spoke to myself. Self-compassion had no place in my life. I never cut myself any slack. I was the most hateful person that I had ever come across, and things couldn't go on like this. I began exercises that I thought were stupid, like looking into my own eyes in the mirror and repeatedly saying, "I love you." The hokey police almost arrested me for that one. It felt so strange and stupid, but that fact alone spoke volumes about how I really felt about myself.

Self-care is a hot buzzword lately, but what does that really look like? It's not all bubble baths and essential oils and drinking water, although that can be some of it. For me, the act of self-love begins with tuning in to where I am emotionally, right now. Do I need to purge the junk food from my pantry? Do I need to force myself to go for a walk instead of vegging out in front of Netflix? Do I need to take a nap in the middle of the day because I didn't sleep well and I am not being truly productive?

Self-care is forgiving yourself for screaming like a banshee at the kids over stupid things like forgetting their keys. It is an out of body moment, seeing outside yourself without judgment. It is saying, "Of course, you are frustrated and tired. You've been strong for a really long time. Let's finish this work, and then I'll take you to the sauna to sweat it out. Here's a nice Caesar salad. It's one of your favorites, and you need the vitamin A."

Women have the hardest time taking care of themselves because you are programmed to take care of everyone else. The truth is, there is only so much effort a human being can put into a single day. If you would adopt the emergency airline tactic of putting on your own mask before helping others, you would be so much better off, but you don't. You give until it hurts, and then you get angry about how empty you feel.

The biggest test of self-love for me is setting appropriate boundaries with everyone in my life. Being insanely codependent in the past has skewed my thinking. I am getting better with this, but I still find myself having to course correct. Lucky for me, I have a man in my life that is a master at setting healthy boundaries. He gently leads me back to center when I veer off course. As I create healthy boundaries, it opens up energy. It opens up space in my mind for myself and for rest. It also requires the people in my life to level up and begin to do the things they should have been doing for themselves all along. Yes, I will forever be the person who lives to make cookies for her kids and looks for ways to take care of people. But having the right boundaries in place helps me get to a place where I can give freely without resentment. Because I have enough left over to love on myself, I also have more to give to the other people in my life. Love isn't like energy, of which there is only so much to go around. Love multiplies, like when you add another child to your family.

Self-love is learning to embrace your individuality, even if you are in a relationship. It is honoring your feelings and emotions enough to be able to speak your mind when things hurt, instead of stuffing it all away. It's easy to let your life morph into someone else's, and I was the queen of wrapping my life around the guy I was with at the expense of my sense of self. The healthier you become, the harder it is to conform against your true self and the easier it is to embrace your entirety. You no longer *need* another person in your life, but you can *choose* to travel alongside someone. It tells you, "Hey, girl, you're gonna be okay no matter what. You've conquered some pretty crazy shit in the past, and I have 100% faith in your ability to do so in the future."

It is not arrogant or selfish to love yourself, either, if pursued in a healthy way. Seeing the bright light you are, seeing the love you have to give, and the gifts you were born to share in the clearest vision possible are all good things. Self-love is evaluating everything that comes into your life with greater clarity because you are coming from a place of love. It is making the hard decisions that fall in line with your values, even when they are difficult or scare you.

When you hate yourself, you choose bad partners, you work at dead-end and unchallenging jobs, you make bad financial decisions, and you eat all the snack cakes. You live in fear—fear of being alone, fear of putting yourself out there, fear of getting rejected, fear of being seen for the gorgeous and vivacious human you are. When you hate yourself, you beat yourself up for mistakes you've made, and on the priority list of life, you put yourself last.

When you love yourself, you walk away from people who tell you it's hard to love you. You go out on a limb to reach for that dream job, you take your body on hikes, and you eat blueberries and salmon and chocolate. When you love yourself, you reflect on your mistakes with self-compassion instead of self-loathing. You give yourself the benefit of the doubt, and you stop holding yourself to an impossible and unobtainable standard.

What does your current experience have to say about how much you love or hate yourself right now? Almost everything is in your life by choice. Truly. Most things don't just happen. You call them to you by the standards you have set and the concessions you have made. Outside of your family of origin and your childhood experiences, as an adult, you are attracting pain or repelling it.

Ask: What does loving yourself look like right now? I can't take credit for this question because it came from one of the millions of podcasts I listened to over the years, but it is so poignant that I wrote it on an index card I tacked above my desk so I can see it every day. Some days, it will be slacking and relaxing, while other days, it will be pushing myself to finish that book. But each day is a day to wake up and find ways to love yourself in all the big and small ways you can find to bring more joy and love into your own life. It is not someone else's job to do that. You have to do it. You have to fill your life with the things you love because then, when a healthy man comes into it, he won't be solely responsible for your happiness and joy. He will add to it, absolutely, but your happiness and joy won't depend completely on him. Putting your happiness and joy solely into the hands of another person is disastrous. It's an impossible task to give another human being. You are the CEO of your own happiness, so start making decisions like a badass, take no prisoners CEO would.

If you are not ready to make huge sweeping changes quite yet, start with something smaller and build on it. Small changes over time can have a huge impact on the future life you will lead. It will also build up your self-love and decision-making muscles, so you can take on scarier and harder decisions that will increase your self-love factor monumentally.

Think about how you treat someone you just fell in love with. You go out of your way to prove it to them. You remember when they mention their favorite candy bar, and you surprise them with one. You cook dinners and give massages and little gifts. You pour all your love onto them. What if you poured all that love you've been pouring on the wrong people onto yourself?

The opposite of self-love, respect, and compassion is self-abuse. Each decision you make should be evaluated during this time, from the food you put in your mouth to the people you invite into your life. Does this support the life I want to live? This is a tedious process that is effort-intensive. It will take time to get momentum to build so that it becomes hard to make unhealthy choices. Keep going.

The only person you will live with forever is yourself. It's time to be nice to her, take her out on the town, and protect her heart and strengthen her soul, body, and mind. You are worth it, so go get your self-love on! (And masturbate if you want to! Orgasms count as self-love, too!)

The Big Takeaway Question: Do you truly love yourself?

Look in the mirror and say, "I love you." If it feels bad or stupid, you just need to do it more. Trust me.

Make a list of everything that is in your life right now. Your job, your friends, your relationships, your hobbies, list everything. Take a complete inventory of where you are right now in life. Next to each item on the list, add a heart for good loving choices and a sad face for horrible life-murdering ones. Try to look at everything that defines you and your life from a third-party perspective. Be completely unemotional about it. If you've got hearts all over it, this book was probably a waste of time for you because you are killing it! But if there are more sad faces there than at a Justin Bieber concert, then it is time to acknowledge this and learn to love yourself.

SELF ABUSE

Abuse is a hateful, painful word, but it's also oh so accurate. When you beat yourself up for mistakes you've made or continually go back in the past and ruminate over things you should have done differently, that is self-abuse. When your self-talk is demeaning and negative, that is a form of self-abuse. When you continuously feed your body with junk, skip the gym, or drink too much, that is a form of self-abuse. When you compare your body to the photoshopped images in magazines in the checkout line, that is a form of self-abuse. When you continue to withhold things you need to be happy—food, love, sleep, forgiveness—that is self-abuse. When you seek out damaged partners who treat you like dirt, take advantage, or use you, that is self-abuse.

When you take self-deprecating to a whole new level, constantly telling others you're an idiot and can't do anything right, that is a form of self-abuse. All it does is show the world how much you hate yourself and how uncomfortable you are in your own skin. It stems from the fear of putting your awesomeness out there for all to see and getting a swift kick in the crotch. You are afraid that you won't be accepted or loved, or you don't believe you deserve to be loved. You are so afraid of the comments and the jokes others might make that you beat people to the punch and tell them before anyone gets a chance, often more cruelly than the other person ever would. Self-abuse is the easiest abuse to participate in because, wherever you go, there you are. You can literally engage in it 24/7.

In the last few years, I finally connected the dots that loving yourself is essential for living in the flow of life. If you don't love yourself, everything else becomes an uphill battle. You sabotage yourself, many times unconsciously because your self-hatred is so strong that your feelings of unworthiness attract things into your life that make it a self-fulfilling prophecy. It's a vicious cycle that continues until you make a conscious effort to change it. By the time you notice, like I did, the track is worn down from years and years of this automatic behavior, so it is difficult to build a newer healthier path. Unless you focus your attention on it, you will continue to live in and draw this kind of pain into your life, and you will struggle. If you don't love yourself, the other good things you want to attract to your life can't be invited in because your lack of self-love keeps them all at bay. It sends out this undermining energy that blocks all the good things you desire.

It has to start with you. It has to start with you deciding to stop the self-abuse. It has to start with you identifying abusive behaviors and then taking steps to correct them. You will be asked to cut people out of your life or eliminate as much contact as possible with family members. The destructive abusive patterns that you have engaged in will have to be broken, and this takes time. It will be easy to get discouraged and fall back into what feels normal to you. You will need to look at this forward and back process with self-compassion, something that most self-abusers don't even know how to do.

Self-compassion should be cultivated in your life as much as possible. You need to stop shaming and blaming yourself and instead see your life as a work in progress that deserves some grace. You deserve patience and room for errors. As you make changes to be kinder to yourself, one way to discover if you have self-compassion is to ask, "Would I say that to my best friend?" If the answer is no, then it is obvious that you need to stop saying those things to yourself, either out loud or in your thoughts. Become your own best friend and speak the words of joy and love into your own heart. Give yourself the benefit of the doubt. When you screw up, forgive yourself for making a mistake. Don't return to it over and over in your head and punish yourself endlessly. No one deserves that form of double jeopardy. You have already done the time. You don't need to wallow in that pit of shame. You have paid your debt already. Forgive yourself and let it go.

It's time to do the work to love yourself and, at first, it will feel stupid and self-indulgent. You might get discouraged because you think nothing is happening, but keep going. Time really is the great equalizer of everything. You will get to a clearing. It will be like climbing a mountain. It will be challenging and slow going, and sometimes seem like you are going in circles. And then, one day, you will get to the summit and the view will be spectacular. You will get to the place in your mind where you have cut out the toxic relationships, which will free more of your resources to focus on other things from your list that make you feel good. You will set up boundaries and learn to lock the cupboards. This will shut down the takers in your life and help you stop over-giving to free up more of your resources. Your calmer mind will open up energy for better uses of your time. You should fill this newly found time with things you love to do. These events will compound, and you will find yourself getting happier and happier.

As you grow happier and happier, you will draw more of what you want and love into your life because it won't be able to help itself. It can't miss you. Lack of self-love blocks everything. If you can just trust and accept this truth, then you will be ready to make the small changes in your day that bring you joy. You will see the magic appear back in your life.

When you are having a bad day, ask, "What does loving myself look like right now?" Sometimes, this will mean taking to your bed with Netflix and cookie dough. Sometimes, this will be a long walk to clear your head. Sometimes, it's cranking the heavy metal in the car and screaming the lyrics. Asking this question puts you in a loving mindset that works so well that I find myself saying it to my partner and my kids when they are struggling. It is a loving act to ask someone what they need in a moment of pain. Often, the answer is as small as a hug. Ask yourself this question when you are hurting, frustrated, or struggling, and then do it.

The Big Takeaway Question: What ways do you self-abuse? What unhealthy habits do you fall back on?

This is a difficult one to admit, but we all do it. Identify places where you hurt yourself with your words, your thoughts, your limiting beliefs, or your physical choices of food, exercise, and sleep. How can you change these behaviors into loving ones?

A PENNY FOR YOUR THOUGHTS? SHOULD BE AT LEAST A DOLLAR

Thoughts are powerful things. Your internal dialogue holds every clue you need to uncover in the quest to find and love yourself. Are you an asshole to yourself? Do you say things like these? *"You're such an idiot. You never learn. You fucked that all up! Way to go, dumbass!"* I used to be the queen of the self-deprecating talk, but after hearing how powerful your internal dialogue is and the truth that thought is the most powerful catalyst for change of them all, I made a conscious effort to stop bashing myself on the daily. And you know what? That was fucking hard! It's amazing how quickly you can slip back into derogatory self-speak without even noticing you are doing it in the first place.

Your thoughts are so powerful. They can supercharge your future or doom it to hell, and the amazing thing is that *you* get to choose *every time*. You get to pick the path with every word you say and every thought that you think. Every choice is a brick in the wall of you. You can build your own magnificent castle or shitty, run-down shack. So, if you are reading this and your life sucks, the very first thing to adjust is your thoughts.

It is changing your mental dialogue to be, *"I am learning something new, and people make mistakes. All that means is I am figuring it out."* Instead of, *"I am an idiot. I'll never get it,"* it's saying, *"I am so glad to have an opportunity to learn this new skill."* It's saying, *"Now I can focus on what I want,"* instead of, *"I'm royally fucked."* Would you say any of those things to friends? The overwhelming answer is hell no. No one speaks to other people the way they speak to themselves. Don't you think you deserve a teaspoon of the sweetness that you reserve bushels of for everyone else?

I've had some unusually unlucky luck. I used to say all the time, "Things never work out for me. I never win. Everyone else has it so much easier." Now, I am conscious of the words I choose. I say things like, "Everything always works out for me. Crazy life experiences bring exciting ideas for my books." I correct myself every time with the words I choose, knowing every single one of them has the power to attract what I want or what I hate.

Downward spirals start with downward thoughts that build and build and suck you down. The energy is like a cyclone, feeding and sustaining itself and sucking you deeper into the dirty and dank scary basement of your life. The opposite is also true. You can spiral up, higher and higher to the roof deck of your life with panoramic views of the ocean. Every thought you think is a choice, up or down, easy or hard, simple or complicated.

Thoughts *are* things. The first time I heard this phrase, I was in my eye-rolling, brand new to meditation phase. I downloaded a meditation exercise to help me sleep and, interspersed through the weird flutey new age music and theta waves that sounded like wounded sea turtles, was a woman chanting, "Your thoughts are things," in her hypnotic voice. It was mesmerizing, and honestly, I felt a bit hokey, but I listened and listened and began to hear the phrase from so many other places that I had to admit there might be one ounce of truth to it. Guru after guru proclaimed this truth, and though I have not achieved guru status, I have to concede to the experts. Thoughts absolutely *are* things.

Recently, a news article caught my eye about some people not having an internal dialogue. I was shocked. I thought everyone had a voice in their head commentating on the minutiae of their life. Mine is a cross between Morgan Freeman and Samuel L. Jackson. "I am never doing that again. Motherfucker! In fact, Ninya did do it again. And a second time, just to be certain." From nearly birth, the harsh internal criticism that I subjected myself to cranked up in the morning and then trailed off at night, eventually, after much tossing and turning, half a dozen cookies, and two blue moons. The idea that not everyone shared in this phenomenon was shocking to me. The voice in my head used to be that judgey mean girl at school who points out flaws, one by one, with glee. With lots of therapy, I was able to kick her out and replace her with a kinder little old lady, like Rose from *The Golden Girls*. A voice that was naive and sweeter with stories to tell, with a side of Sophia, a no-nonsense smart ass from Sicily.

Take inventory of the voices in your head. Was your dad an abusive asshole who emotionally or physically destroyed you? If you grew up with the bullshit of others on repeat in your head, you will need to clean and clear that out. It will be harder to remove this brainwashing because it comes from an outside source. Sadly, most people put far more stock in what others say about them, especially someone in a position of perceived authority. Work with a therapist to address these falsehoods. It will be a sound investment in your healing and worth every penny.

Wherever your thoughts originated, they can be used to punish yourself and keep you imprisoned. Your mind is the most powerful part of your body. Harnessing the power of it is something that takes a lifetime to learn and needs constant recalibration. When you make the shift and start using your mind to love yourself, things begin to change quickly. You will see opportunities where you once saw obstacles. You will see potential where you used to see a dead end. Life becomes a joyful journey again instead of a painful tale of woe. It all starts with your thoughts. The beauty of this is that thoughts are free. Anyone, regardless of economic background, race, or sex, can develop this part of their life and benefit from it. There is no barrier to entry, and no one gets special treatment or privilege. For once we are all taking off from the same starting line.

Your thoughts are powerful internal voices that you can harness for good or evil. Choose now to use them for good. Retrain your brain to speak light and truth into your heart and see how fast things will begin to shift. It is magic, and it is something anyone can do right now, regardless of your current life circumstances. Thought is the great equalizer. Harnessing its power can completely transform your life.

The Big Takeaway Question: What is your internal dialogue saying?

If you are unsure what you say to yourself, take a day to pay attention. When your internal dialogue cranks up, write down what it says. Instead of walking through life on autopilot, tune in to your internal frequency, and make notes about what you hear. Report it without bias. Re-write any negatives and limiting thoughts with its positive opposite. These will become great mantras to repeat to yourself when your inner critic starts her monologue because that bitch never knows when to shut up. Better yet, replace her with someone sweeter, someone who loves you.

THE LESSONS YOU NEED TO LEARN

The most painful transition I have ever faced happened in 2018. My entire life was burned down to the ground, and I struggled to find my way. It was almost laughable, the series of events that happened, and I marveled at the power of the universe.

"Oh, you have trust issues? Here are ten photos and a video of your new boyfriend posted to Facebook, doing shots while surrounded by pretty girls all night at the bar after he blew you off the day you were laid off to avoid the drive to your house."

"Is security your greatest fear? Let's take away not one, but two sources of income and see how you handle that. You know what? On second thought, let's just take them all, so there is no income at all. Oh, and let's see what you do now that you have a kid who relies on your every move so they can eat."

"Oh, people take advantage of you? Let's send more, but this time make them total strangers that cross every line and ask for crazy things. Surely, you will tell them to go straight to hell."

What a sense of humor this beautiful life seems to have. The lessons you need to learn are custom made and sent to you repeatedly, and with greater intensity, until you have no recourse but to take heed and learn. The stakes get higher. What first starts as a whisper becomes a scream so loud and terrifying, it crowds out everything else.

If ignored, life can become a punishing taskmaster. You don't get to say, *"No, thank you."* You are forced to sit still and learn the lessons, no matter what. There are no free passes or get out of jail cards. There is only the acceptance of the lesson. It's up to you how much you will choose to fight it. Being stubborn and looking the other way will only prolong the inevitable. It's best to just dig in and eat that shit sandwich the first time, and with a smile on your face, or you will be asked to eat two.

Life is creative, bringing endless exercises to drive home the same point until you understand. Pain is never for nothing. There is always a seed of something in it that is for your benefit. There is always something that will help you grow and become more, but the lessons can be excruciating. I think life chooses pain to reinforce the hardest lessons so that you never forget. If you don't have some degree of suffering, you won't retain the lesson near as well.

Start by asking the problem, "What are you here to teach me?" instead of retreating into martyr mode. Asking this question helps you regain control of your thinking. If you search out the value of the lesson, you can clearly see the personal flaws that need to be healed and addressed. You can see you are jealous, or insecure, or hurt. Then you can choose to take action to heal those parts of yourself and give yourself security, stability, and love. You can cultivate the things in your life that are lacking instead of expecting someone else to do it for you.

The Big Takeaway Question: What lessons keep resurfacing for you?

Learn to tune in to the lessons life is trying to teach you. Learn to hear the whisper instead of the scream. What pain is in your life right now? What is this pain trying to teach you?

THE MOST IMPORTANT RENOVATION PROJECT

I have always loved a good home improvement project. Pulling into the parking lot at Lowe's or Home Depot gets me giddy. It is the transformation process that I am in love with, taking something boring or unattractive and making it more functional and prettier. I've extensively remodeled every house I've ever lived in, and the never-ending projects kept me busy. So busy that remodeling became a distraction, so I didn't have to focus on the fact that I had married the wrong person. The constant busywork of choosing colors and flooring and sink placement kept most of my mind occupied, so I had little resources left for the things that needed to change in my life—the stuff that would actually matter.

I was unhappy but also unwilling to look at the real root cause of the unhappiness, and so I continued fixing up house after house when what I really needed to do was fix myself. The disconnect was so substantial, and I was in such denial. As each project completed, there would be a temporary sense of satisfaction that quickly died, and then I was off to chase another high, this time with heated floors.

Brazilian Cherry was not going to make me happy, but I didn't see that. Making the surfaces beautiful didn't repair the vast ugliness that was waiting inside. I had wallpapered layer after layer over my soul until the seams were starting to come apart, but each time a crack appeared, I would spackle that bitch shut so fast it was mind-blowing. This was exhausting, tail-chasing work that left me depleted at the end of the day. The kind of exhausted where you fall into bed fully clothed and fall asleep immediately, with no time to think about anything before you drift off.

I never saw this pattern of behavior for what it was until after we had relocated to a Des Moines suburb. The public reason for our move was that there were better opportunities for our artistic children. The honest reason was that I just couldn't stand to really see that my life wasn't working, and the best thing to do at the time was to completely fill my mind with the logistics of moving my family of four two hours away. We moved so much during that period, six times in four years, that I got exceptionally good at the process. Working out the most efficient way to do it was completely mind monopolizing.

If I had just directed my focus inside instead of focusing on making the outside beautiful, things would have taken a much different road. I was afraid to face the truth that I wanted a divorce. I was afraid to face the idea of breaking up my family. I was afraid to face the fact that I wasted decades with the wrong person who couldn't give me what I needed, not because he didn't want to, but because his addictions made him unable.

When I finally faced the facts and understood what I was doing, it was a hard reality to swallow because I had wasted so much time, effort, and money in this process. I finally got a therapist and began remodeling my mind. One session was all it took to uncover massive structural work that needed to be done, work that would take time and effort to bring everything up to code. Emotionally, I was jacked up.

The process of healing yourself is oddly similar to a renovation. You literally have to gut yourself, your thought patterns, your emotions, your relationships with every significant person in your life. You have to tear everything down to the studs with sledgehammers and crowbars. It is soul-crushing, painful work, which is why many people refuse to do it. They decide to live with the toxic mold secretly growing behind the Venetian plastered walls, believing that as long as I can't see it, it doesn't exist. I, too, lived in this denial for years. Living in my structurally unsound, emotional body, deemed uninhabitable for others but good enough for me. Through therapy, I peeled away layer after layer of toxic asbestos wallpaper, each layer needing a more delicate touch to prevent further damage. Then, one day, I discovered that I was hiding hardwood floors underneath all that seventies shag carpet, and it was such an unexpected diamond of a find that it gave me the boost I needed to keep going.

I am healthier now. I say this because I truly feel this is something you work on forever. You continue to change and grow and manage your life, and the problems that arise bring even more reno projects to light that need to be worked on. Looking over the entirety of my life, seeing where I came from and where I am now is like looking at the before and after photos of a whole-house renovation. In a glance, you can see where you were and how far you have come. It is truly a wonder to behold, the changes that can happen to completely transform a person.

You are your most important renovation project. You have everything you need inside you that might be covered under layers of ugliness and pain. You are worth the time and energy it takes to create a lighter and fully restored emotional body. This is your most important work. This is the one renovation that will truly change your life if you are bold enough to do it. It won't happen overnight, but when you take a step back and revel in the magic of where you started and where you are now, there is not a more satisfying feeling in the entire world.

The Big Takeaway Question: What are you remodeling mentally, spiritually, or emotionally right now?

You change constantly. I know that if you look back at yourself ten years ago, you have made massive changes in a decade. The constant quest of becoming more in tune with your soul is a never-ending one. Journal on what soul shifts you want or need to make that would make your life better and more fulfilling. What projects should you undertake right now?

BE A FINISHER

Finish what you start. My dad was a Marine. During bootcamp, they indoctrinated him with pillars of integrity and military values and rebuilt him from the ground up. One of those pillars was "You must finish what you start." Lucky me, being the daughter of a Marine, he held me to these same standards. Quitting was never an option.

As I have gotten older and wiser, I have added this caveat--- only finish things that are healthy. I am not advocating staying stuck in an abusive marriage because you made a vow. I am urging you to be an advocate for your betterment. Do not continue to toil in dead-end jobs or dead-end relationships because you don't want to be a quitter. Sometimes, you have to quit something that you committed to because, in the greater scheme of things, it doesn't fit your new authentic life. Letting go of these things that are not meant for you may be very difficult and come with a lot of emotions like guilt and anger. Above all else, let your desire for complete health—body, mind, and soul—dictate your decisions.

But when it comes to healthy pursuits, if you are stalling

out, consider this. Starting is always the easiest part. On the heady high of change, the daydream of how things are going to be different once you have completed the lofty goal propels you forward. Day three seems to be the worst, when the pain of giving up the bad habit is at its peak and the bad habit becomes easy to slide back into. That familiar place you know so well nearly feels like home. Life is so good at getting in the way of you and your ambitious goal. It throws up so many roadblocks and detours, and most people get lost or abandon the project altogether at that point.

Finishing things is hard and takes effort. That's why people stay stuck being overweight, in unhappy marriages, and with books half-written. It's so easy to quit and let go of the struggle. But these people, even when they quit, likely don't quit all the way. They are the ones that have the affair instead of ending the marriage. They get distracted by something that takes the pain away, even temporarily, instead of bearing down and gritting through the hard middle, where your mind plays tricks on you and tells you that you weren't good enough to start this in the beginning. That things for you will never work out. So, you reach for something that feels good in whatever flavor you crave—wine, shopping, sex, cake, even drugs, anything to make the pain of what you are currently going through stop. The ways we soothe ourselves are infinite and personal. We are all weak-kneed when these pain killers come calling.

Abandoning goals and projects becomes a habit, too, one that is an infidelity to yourself. With those little self-sabotaging behaviors, you are saying to yourself, *"You are not worth this effort. You are not worth this temporary pain. You can't finish this. You don't deserve this. Settle."*

I once had a friend who had been demolishing her house for years. I called it demolishing, but she liked to call it remodeling. Read on to see which you feel was more accurate. Every time a new project would start up, she'd be slightly crazed with excitement, showing me photos of the dramatic after transformation she was shooting for, and over several years she became a pro at demolition. Knee-deep in lathe and plaster, she'd wipe the dust from her goggles and continue, but more often than not, she'd hit a roadblock, like important wiring in a wall she was trying to remove, or complex tile cuts she didn't trust herself to do, and the fear made her stall out. The project would sit, unfinished, sometimes for years as she would continue to live her life around it. Completely inconvenienced yet still willing to tear up another section of her house when the mood struck again. I couldn't do it. Having to stare at the half-done projects and live in rubble day after day would kill me. It would wear on my brain that craves simple and easy. My newly minimalistic mind would sit in the corner and rock itself, unable to cope, let alone rest in a home that was in a constant state of destruction.

Many times, when you tear up the world around you, there is a deeper cry for help. It can become a metaphor for your life. The disorganization and destruction can be a visual representation of the state of your mind. It is heartbreaking how pain manifests physically in our lives, one way or another. Finishing the abandoned projects is a way you can reclaim your brain cells to focus on other things instead of letting your brain become preoccupied and distracted.

Finishing is hard. It's not sexy. It's sucking it up at times and finding the courage to continue. It's ending something before beginning the next. It puts your brain in a state of peace instead of stress. When you complete things, you are building finishing muscles. You are teaching yourself and others that you mean what you say, that you finish what you start, and that you back up your words with actions. Over time, you build your finishing muscles to the point that not finishing becomes painful. Like those insane people who say skipping the gym is more painful than going. I kid, but not really. It becomes a new pattern, a new way of thinking, and a new way of being.

People who finish have integrity. They are dependable. You can trust them to do what they say. Being dependable is a rare quality these days and one that you should work to develop. Discipline is especially important when the right thing to do is hard, when the healthy choice takes effort and sacrifice. Finishing things will give you a sense of accomplishment. It will fill you with pride that you persevered. So, whatever is unfinished in your life right now, dig deep and finish it.

The Big Takeaway Question: What is unfinished in your life right now? What have you completed?

Journal about both of these, the wins and the losses. Pick one unfinished project and outline steps you need to take to finish this one project. Cross each step off as you complete it. This act gives the brain a hit of dopamine when you accomplish something, even something seemingly small. Focus on this one unfinished task until it is completed, then celebrate in a small way before tackling the next one.

Visualize the big things you have finished in the past. Remember the feeling of accomplishment you felt. Let it wash over you again so you understand why you need to finish in the first place.

There is power in the action of completion. You will build momentum and prove to yourself that you mean what you say. That when you promise to do something, you show up, even if it's hard. Finish these projects and free your mind for bigger things.

WELL-ROUNDED

One of the biggest lies you are spoon-fed from birth is that a person needs to be well-rounded. Schools are amazing at softening your edges, like rocks in a tumbler, making them all a uniform soft and silky-smooth surface. It's easier for people to walk all over smooth rocks than it is for them to walk all over the sharpened ones.

I think that way of thinking is bullshit. I think you should go 1000% the other way. Sharpen those edges like a sword. Find the one thing that sets you apart and sharpen that blade so it cuts anything it encounters into ribbons.

Society loves to put people in boxes, to categorize and sift and sort. My parents, great people though they were, bought into this lie wholeheartedly and, as a result, told me to become an accountant. Me! Or a lawyer! Laughable. I am the least argumentative person you will ever meet. I'm the very definition of live and let live. Both of these things would have supported me, likely very well monetarily, but the bigger cost was my happiness and my soul. In the eighties, it was more important to teach your children to chase the security of a stable job. The problem is that the stable job no longer exists. Companies, for the most part, are no longer loyal, cutting the fat at the drop of a hat. Currently, in the middle of a pandemic, companies are cutting to the bone, and unemployment is at record levels. There is no such thing as getting a good job and then working there for the next thirty years of your life and retiring. These types of opportunities do not exist. Corporate greed has squeezed them out. Now, it is about performing and hitting the benchmarks like a college football coach. If you don't put enough W's in the win column, there are ten thousand other candidates at the ready to jump in and take over at a moment's notice.

College well-rounds the hell out of you, forcing you to get a two-year General Education degree before you get to the good stuff and take classes that have anything to do with your major. Tens of thousands of dollars later, you have earned the right. Personally, unless you need a specialized degree or certificate, like to become a doctor or lawyer, I think that college is the biggest waste of time and an even bigger waste of money. I have always thought that, which is the reason I only got a vocational technical degree. College was another lie and another trap that the world built for you to fall into and imprison you further. My generation was told to go to college so you'll get a good job. Many of us bought into that lie and mortgaged our future to the hilt. Some of us, even now in our forties, still have college debt we are struggling to pay off. As a result, we have been chained to the grind, that nine to five job that fills our checking account, but not our soul.

Being well-rounded is a result of the day to day settling that occurs in your life. It's spending time outside your sphere of genius and is actually very detrimental to the development of your true gifts. This is not to say you should limit yourself to only things that sharpen your sword. That is not true. What I am asking you to do is cut the obligatory things, the tasks you force yourself to do, the hoops that you jump through for other people. Instead, spend that time following your curiosity, wherever it leads, in playful and serious sessions. If something sounds like fun or piques your interest, chase it and see where it goes. Sometimes, it leads nowhere, but you might find that it is deeply connected to your purpose. No matter what, curiosity is the key. Follow it and you might see another part of your true self emerge, instead of forcing down the obligation and wasting your time doing the things other people expect you to do.

Steve Jobs wasn't well-rounded, nor were Salvador Dali and Michael Jordan. Any uber successful person at the top of their game is singularly focused. They are tuned in to themselves and the gift they were sent to give to the world. They get up every day and sharpen their sword in their area of greatness until it can shred with ease. They become lightning rods, charged with their own genius, attracting and harnessing the electricity of the world in that one pinpointed area. Electricity has no choice but to strike them over and over because they have decided. They have built a beacon for their thing. Their one true thing. Sharp and high above the others, lightning physically cannot pass them by.

Well-rounded is for pussies. Sharpen that sword. Build that lightning rod.

The Big Takeaway Question: What is your one true thing? What do you do out of obligation that you need to let go?

What is your sphere of genius? Discover your one true thing. Do this by analyzing the questions you answered from the first chapter. Give yourself permission to continue to grow and excel in the areas you enjoy and succeed at naturally. Let go of the tasks that weigh you down, that don't interest you, and that you do out of obligation.

Focus all of your effort and energy on the things that you are called to do. If your career is wrong and doesn't fit your gifts, outline the steps you need to take to move toward your genius. The average person changes careers five to seven times in their lifetime. Plot a plan for an escape that allows you to move toward the new while still taking care of your current responsibilities.

YOUR INTUITION KNOWS. LISTEN

Trusting your intuition should be simple and easy. You know those feelings you have that make your skin crawl or get you excited? Those are messages from your intuition. The problem is that it's easy to ignore intuition in favor of logic. Even skewed logic is favored over intuition.

Logic is the asshole heckler in the back of the comedy club. He's the voice that tells you to go to college when really you want to write the book and travel. Logic tells you this guy is good enough because you will never find everything you want in one person. Logic says you are lucky to have this soul-sucking job with health insurance. Logic scans the room for potential problems, finds the path of least resistance, and then calculates it against acceptable payoff and conspires to keep you stuck in mediocrity. Logic is the path to okayness. Everything is okay. This is good enough. Let's settle.

Intuition is logic's sexy cousin, who smokes dope and wears flowing caftans. She floats through life and owns who she is, and she doesn't dare apologize for it. She is naturally at ease, so in tune with herself that she breezes through life, throwing up no resistance and laughing her throaty laugh all the way home. Intuition tells you the sky is the limit, dream big, follow your gut and let go. Intuition says anything is possible. It is the path to your happy place.

Intuition wants to give you the people and experiences that gel with who you are and what you want, but sometimes intuition tells you to do things that are outside your norm, so logic pipes up and says, "Whoa, Nelly! You can't do that or have that. You have responsibilities. How about you compromise and do this instead? It is safer with a guarantee of 27% satisfaction." So, you often choose the safe route, even though it will make your life less fulfilling. If you had just listened, you could have flowed into a life that fits you. But you are afraid and paralyzed by fear. It's easier to not do anything than to step out and trust your intuition to guide you and do the crazy things it's asking you to do.

If you put too much weight on logic, your life becomes a series of settlings that collectively impact you, and that is where the midlife crisis is born. You might think that one little logical decision is fine, but added up and compounded over time, they completely change the trajectory of your life. Instead of ending up in sunny Paris, you're in a dirty alley in Hell's Kitchen.

There is an underlying energy to everything. Everything is connected. To tap into this energy, you just need to relax, trust, and be open to where your intuition leads you. Trusting is usually where you'll struggle because that requires you to let go when you are used to white-knuckling it. It is discovering what your true nature is and accepting it fully. It is relaxing into the deepest expression of your own truthful existence and being confident enough to follow intuition where she leads.

Last night, I went to dinner with friends where we had an impromptu tarot card reading, and I drew the High Priestess, considered the most intuitive card in the deck, the gateway between the conscious and subconscious mind. I guess the universe is sending me the bat signal that I still have a lot of work to do in this arena. I am at a crossroads in my life professionally right now, and I know in my heart I am a writer. I know this is the place I need to focus and place my intention and effort, so every morning, I sit down and crank out pages. Some pages are great, but many of them are so terrible and cringe-worthy I banish them forever with my often used delete key. Pursuing this dream feels so right and natural to me, my intuition is telling me this is my path. She is saying this is what I need to do with my life, and so I will continue down this road, take the next step she sends me, and see where that leads.

I am trying to clamp my hand over logic's mouth when he says, "There are a million writers out there already. What is the chance that you will be able to actually have people pay to read anything you write?" He's loud and obnoxious and tells me what I want is too risky. I have kids to feed. I've mastered the art of redirection, so I continue to walk down my path toward what I believe is my gift. Some days, I skip down it, and some days, I'm constantly looking over my shoulder for bandits on the road. I wish I could say that it is easy, but it's not. That is kind of the point.

Trusting your intuition means getting in touch with who you naturally are, free from what others want you to be. What do you love to do? What makes you feel energized and excited? What spreads a smile so big on your face it makes your cheeks hurt? Walk toward more of that. It sounds like the simplest thing in the world, but it's often the most difficult because we factor other people's thoughts, feelings, and reactions into it. STOP. It's YOUR intuition. Follow her because she is never wrong. She may lead you down the weirdest, windiest paths, but eventually, you will open up to an amazing place that fills you with such personal joy and peace and feels so right.

The Big Takeaway Question: Are you tuned in to your intuition?

List some times in your life where you listened to your gut, where you had a feeling and went with it. What did that gut instinct feel like? What were the outcomes of following it? List some other times where you went against your intuition. What were those outcomes?

GET IN THE FLOW

There are two approaches to life. One is gentle and flowing. It's getting in the water on your inner tube with your case of beer attached to the tube next to you and floating down the river. Letting the current pull you gently down the path of life until you reach your take-out point where you are greeted by a friendly guide who offers you a bus ride back and nachos. Or you can choose the other, where you fight against the current, swallowing most of the lake and choking on it until you finally reach the shore completely exhausted. Which one sounds more enjoyable?

My ex had a friend named Scot. Whatever Scot needed showed up at the perfect time, every single time. He seemed to be in complete alignment with everything. If he had to move, his new employer provided a moving company to pack up and unload every single possession he owned. If he needed a job, he would magically get a job offer at the exact right time, doing something he loved for a lot more money than his current position. It was magical and jealousy-inducing to watch from the sidelines. He was fully in the flow.

When it was time for us to move from the small town we were living in to be closer to our photography clients, we looked to find the right home to buy so we could run a business out of it. We searched for almost three years and found the perfect set-up. It had a huge yard that could be landscaped for photos. It had a walkout basement facing the front of the house, which was weird for most people, but for us was perfect because the lower level was our studio, gallery, and consultation area. To have people be able to walk into that area without coming through the rest of the house when you have an infant and a toddler was a dream come true. We put in an offer contingent on the sale of our current house, and then twenty-four hours later, someone made a contingent free offer. I remember being so sad as I saw the dream of the perfect house drifting away. We had to have an offer on our current house in forty-eight hours or we would lose the perfect house. We showed it only four times, and out of nowhere, an offer came in at the perfect time that allowed us to step into this better space. The pieces all fell into place at just the right time. It was truly an in the flow moment.

How do you get in the flow? You stop. You stop wanting it so badly. You stop the desperation of wanting the thing you think you need so much. You step out into faith that what you need is coming. It is easy to have a one-track mind when consumed with the want to have something, someone, or for some situation to line up in your life. What this really does is constrict things so tightly, creating so much tension that the gifts the universe is trying to give you get stopped. The wanting kills the flow. I have learned this lesson so fully that when I write my yearly goals now, I always leave room for the flow. I set a financial goal and then add the words "or more" because, if the universe wants to be my sugar daddy, who am I to stand in its way? It is the art of leaving space for something even better. It is setting an intention, the destination you want to go, and then letting it go.

I someday want to make an extraordinary income by selling my books so I can live the life I want to live and contribute the way I want to contribute. It is hard when I feel the pressure to complete a book and then take on the task of marketing it and selling it. I am visualizing the life I will live when my books are successful. I vividly imagine strolling on the beach with my guy. Seeing my kids laughing and loving their lives. I see the donations I can make to causes that will actually use the money for the cause and not an inflated board of directors. I can see my passport filling up with stamps, and I see and almost feel the beautiful home I have always wanted to build, right down to the marble island in the huge kitchen that's flooded with light.

For the most part, envisioning this life is very productive. It keeps me on task and pushes me to write on days where I feel less than creative. I see all of this every morning, and then I let it go. It's a process to find the right balance to be focused on what you want while, at the same time, being open to the flow. I am getting better at less laser focusing and more finding the path of least resistance to the place I want to end up. I know where I want to go. I have set my destination with the universe, and now I need to relax and get in the flow. I need to trust that God will show up in his canoe, and the inner GPS will crank up, and even if we get rerouted, He knows where I want to end up and will find a way to get me there or to someplace even better.

Flow is simple and easy and yet one of the most difficult things to surrender to because it requires giving up control. You think you have the power to control your life, but you really don't. It's a false sense of control. If you are not on the right path, the rocks come rushing toward you, and you bash yourself against them trying to swim upstream when all you really need to do is relax and let the current pull you to where it wants you to go. Nature always works. Nature is simple and perfect, and its timing is always impeccable. Fighting against that only exhausts you internally and depletes your resources. Stop the fight and enter the flow. Life is so much better here.

The Big Takeaway Question: Do you fight or flow?

Journal about the instances in your life where things just fell into place, where everything you needed appeared at the perfect time. Contrast that with an uphill battle you have waged. What can be learned in the contrast of these two instances?

UNLUCKY

I used to be unlucky. The kind of girl whose reservation was always lost and whose plans always fell through. I planned a trip to New Orleans with girlfriends a couple of years ago, and a week before our flight was scheduled to land, our VRBO host went MIA. Literally zero contact or response to messages, he went off the grid—silent. Over the course of several ignored messages, the anxiety increased, proving that I was unlucky yet again, but this time, I had three other people I was responsible for in the mix. Typical. That's what I told myself. Nothing ever goes my way.

My guy said it will all work out, to just call the company and see what the options are, so I did. And within twenty-four hours, we were settled into a brand new condo, closer to the French Quarter, upgraded with more bedrooms and gorgeous bathrooms, and it was absolutely free since VRBO refunded almost our entire first reservation. I was in shock. This was not the way things usually worked out for me.

There is a woman in my former neighborhood who wins everything. She wins trips to the Caribbean on a yearly basis, her husband was on *Wheel of Fortune* and won a huge jackpot, and she has called into the *Kelly and Ryan Live* show more than once and won. I have never in my entire life met another person with such amazing luck. She believes she will, so she does. It cranks up the jealousy monster that loves to say shitty things like, "That's so unfair. Her life is already a cakewalk. How about the universe spread some of that this direction?"

Her energy is, *I am lucky*, and so financial windfalls and gorgeous travel destinations literally fall into her lap. My energy was, *Nothing ever works out for me. I have the worst luck, and so things literally fall apart for me*. I am working hard to change that line of thinking. I am rewriting my internal dialogue to say, *Everything always works out for me*. Something I chant like a monk in my head when I feel a downward spiral pulling me down. Negativity is like an undertow, powerful and consuming. I fight to swim away, but sometimes it takes me down, and instead of fighting it, I have to use chants and walks and re-centering exercises to remain calm and then break free.

I think we are all giant magnets, attracting opportunities and people into our lives according to what we believe. The problem is the frequency you are tuned in to. Once again, the biggest block is in your own mind. Your mind wants you to play small and be safe. Be like my former neighbor. Believe you are going to win, and you just might attract enough positivity that you will.

The Big Takeaway Question: Do you feel lucky?

Take your lucky temperature. Do you feel lucky, or are you more of a doom and gloomer? Change your mindset and see what four leaf clovers pop into your life.

CODEPENDENT MUCH?

After my divorce, it was pretty apparent there was a fair amount of work to do that I had put off for decades. Much like an emotional hoarder, I shoved things into the closet and stuffed things down that I didn't want to deal with. As a result, I had the emotional equivalent of a house packed to the rafters, complete with flat cats. It was a mess, and one I didn't really want to face because of all the same reasons.

Where do I even start? This job is so big, let's just eat some caramels and watch TV. That will make us feel better. Let me buy that shiny thing to distract me from the dumpster fire that had become my life.

Nothing was working, and I was in therapy...again. During a session, my therapist asked if I had read a book called *Codependent No More: How to Stop Controlling Others and Start Caring for Yourself* by Melody Beattie. Intrigued, but thinking she was way off base, I downloaded it anyway and began to read late that night. I am a speed reader and, cover to cover, it took me five hours to read it all. I vividly remember staying up until nearly dawn. The soft light of the iPad was the only light in the room as I swiped and swiped, while this eerie sense of knowing seeped inside me. I bet this is what Adam felt like after he took a bite of Eve's apple. The blinders were off, my soul was naked, everything fell away, and I was not prepared for what I learned.

It was like I had been handed an owner's manual to my life, and the exact reasons and evidence of why things weren't working were laid out for me in rich detail in black and white. It was overwhelming. For the first time, my eyes were wide open and I understood things about myself like I never had before. Until that point, I felt like I was just going through the motions in life, but reading that book shined the spotlight of truth on my life in such a way that I saw everything with complete understanding for the first time ever.

I was married to an alcoholic for sixteen years. People with addictions seem to attract people who will make their lives easier, and that was definitely the case with us. I was not a victim, but he played his part and I played mine. I strived to create a normal life for us and for our family while it allowed his addiction to continue to grow in private. He was a functional alcoholic, which I think is the hardest one to treat because the rest of his life worked to a certain extent, and his addiction could continue under the radar. I was the master of making things work on the surface. He was practically helpless in all areas outside of creating art, but that was okay because that was where I shined. I dove into over-helping him when we had only been dating a few weeks. I helped him get his finances under control because I was eager to prove my loyalty and become important to this man that I loved. He played the powerless and grateful card well, and I was a genius at playing the caretaking, capable one. And so, this sick dynamic was born. To continue a pattern, you need both players, and we both showed up and played our roles hard, almost to death.

NINYA

I never even knew what codependence really meant until that book. I thought it meant I was dependent on him when that was not the case at all. I did all the things to keep all the plates spinning. If anything, he was dependent *on me*. Reading that book, I discovered codependence means doing for another person the things they should be doing for themselves. It is over-giving, over-involvement, trying to control the outcome of another person's decisions and life. It is exhausting to tie up your own mind and resources doing things for fully capable human beings. He never got to hit rock bottom because I softened his landing like *Elasti-girl* on crack, completely stretching and morphing into a sail to land him at rock bottom softly and safely. I wore myself out, trying to protect my family and keep it intact, and in the process, I got in the way of him experiencing the consequences of his choices.

This is not to say I am a saint because I also learned that it puts you in a dangerous giving and resentment cycle that makes you feel taken advantage of, that you actually *give to get*. When your effort isn't reciprocated, you become petty and angry. That was a bitter pill to swallow because I had painted the picture in my mind of what I was giving in the relationship as a little closer to Mother Theresa. After discovering this was a lie, I was ashamed. For a long time, I struggled to accept this truth about myself. I argued internally, "I'm not petty. I am just a giver. Anyone would be unhappy if their partner wasn't putting in the same kind of effort." The unshakable reality was that my gifts always came with strings, and zero reciprocation would put me in a state of anger and frustration. No one wants to be that guy, but I was that guy. It was my go-to character.

Then the real work began. Codependent patterns become so ingrained in you and so automatic that you first have to step back to truly see what you are doing. When you are locked into this behavior for years, it is hard to stop. I found that a gentle third party can sometimes help you see things as they truly are. Then it is up to you to start to make the changes, and that is an arduous process. It will take time to create new boundaries and develop new thought patterns, and then you must brace for the inevitable frustrations from the other party. When you finally stop the over-helping, the over-caretaking, and let them take care of themselves, they will fight back to keep you in the old dynamic. They will call you selfish and try to manipulate you to get you to go back to fixing things in their lives. This is where you need to really take a stand for yourself. You are retraining yourself and them in how things are going to be from now on, and the essential first commandment is "Thou shall be consistent." You must learn to set consistent boundaries and fight against their encroachment.

The second commandment is "Thou shall pause." I found that codependent relationships with addicts are full of drama and a never-ending circus of craziness. If you allow it, their crises will totally take over your life and use all of your life force. Hitting pause will help in so many ways. Don't pick up the phone every time they call. Don't rush to their rescue to help with every little problem. Don't take over because you could do it faster or easier. Learn to let them struggle. Learn to let them fend for themselves. Just like you are flexing your healthy muscles for breaking this dynamic, they need to build up their own healthy muscles in coping with life skills. It will hurt you both for a while. It will be hard on both of you. It will be easy to backstep and revert to the ways you have always done things. Space and time will help everything. Nearly everything can wait for twenty-four hours, even when they call you from jail to bail them out of a mess of their own making. They can wait, in a cell with nothing but time to think about the consequences of the actions that got them there.

Breaking the cycle of codependency is incredibly hard with a spouse, but it is even more difficult with a child. It is so hard to see them fail, to watch them make bad decisions, knowing you could swoop in and save the day. The urge to protect your children is written in your DNA.

I struggled to learn this with my son. Being codependent already with my ex-husband for almost two decades, it was so automatic, I just thought I was mothering. But one day, something shifted, and I realized that I was more concerned about his problem than he was, and yet he had all the power in whether this problem would stop or continue. I was stuck in this sick power exchange that was depleting me on every level, and yet I called it loving him. It was my job. It was my duty as his mother. After much therapy and learning, I started to make small changes that seemed selfish. At first, he rebelled and sucked me back into his drama circus constantly. As time went on and I pursued my own mental health, I was able to put up more healthy boundaries, take more time to respond, and not take responsibility for his decisions knowing he should be doing that on his own. It is something that I am much better at and that I continue to practice. I am grateful I have amazing people in my life who can tell me kindly, "Hey, that's not your problem," or, "You're doing it again," in a nonjudgmental way but that shocks me into re-centering and getting back on track.

It takes time to unlearn healthy behaviors and then put them into practice by doing. It's soul-sucking work that is fraught with guilt. I was raised Catholic, so we have a ton of guilt in our factory settings already, but it comes down to this. How much of your life and energy are you willing to just give way to someone else? How hard are you willing to let life get before you cut yourself free from the patterns that are killing you? Are you helping by over-helping? Are you weakening the other person with your own desire to control? How different could your life look if you focused on yourself and let go of the things that you can't control? It doesn't mean that you accept or condone their behavior, it just means that you didn't create this problem and it is not yours to solve.

The Big Takeaway Question: Are you codependent?

I highly recommend reading *Codependent No More*, especially if you are in a relationship with anyone with an addiction. It truly changed my life. Codependency also rears its head when raising children. If you are a mother, what ways can you help your children develop healthy life skills? What ways can you transfer more of the responsibilities onto their shoulders by teaching them how to become responsible for themselves? When met with a crisis, practice the pause and journal the feelings.

THE CODEPENDENT'S CUPBOARD

Even after reading *Codependent No More*, I struggled to learn this lesson. I wish I could tell you that reading one book would solve your problems in life, but the truth is that understanding yourself is a process and takes many steps. To illustrate this further, I wanted to share one more powerful concept, the codependent's cupboard, that was so enlightening it blew my mind.

I had finished my therapy with one provider and started working with an energy healer. During our initial stunning therapy revelation, my new therapist said to me, "People in your life take everything from you. Imagine your cupboards are open, and they come in and take everything. If there is a single crumb left, they come back and take that, too."

Calling all Mother Hubbards out there. This one is the most difficult lesson for the codependent to master, but when you do, it will completely transform your life. Women are groomed from birth to be caretakers and to self-sacrifice. If you are attached to an addict in a codependent relationship, you are paired up with a taker. My ex-husband was a taker, not because he has a bad bone in his body, but because addiction by itself is selfish. His addiction required someone to look after him and to make his life easier. As a twenty-something with the love goggles on, I stepped up and waved my hands in the air, screaming, "Me! Pick me!!" My lack of experience told me the lie that, if I became indispensable and he needed me, then he must love me when, in reality, it was the furthest thing from the truth. If you were a taker within a hundred-mile radius, I was drawn to you like a moth to a flame. The pattern of giver and taker was all I was used to, and so I sought it out over and over again.

My emotional resources were like a house in the middle of Chicago without a door. "Come on in! See all goodies? Come and get you some! Oh no, you don't owe me anything, nothing at all. Just happy to help. Oh, you owe me money? Don't worry, you can have forever to pay me back."

All that did was leave me in a constant state of emptiness that was difficult to understand. Why do I feel so depleted? Why do I feel so exhausted and empty? A lot of journaling and another session later, I was told to padlock the door. To chain it up and give no one access so I could conserve my own resources to heal myself. Lock it down, so when I was hungry and needed a sammich, the bread wasn't all gone.

At first, this felt very strange and selfish, and I struggled to lock the door and keep it shut. Eventually, you have to concede to trying something new when what you are currently doing clearly isn't working. I decided to give it a try and drew a hard line in the sand. I had gotten to the place where I was done doing things for others that they could do on their own. I was done trying to find solutions for people who weren't willing to do the work themselves, and I was done with giving everything away and getting nothing back.

When you reclaim your life and decide to keep your resources for yourself, if you can push through the initial bouts of selfishness, on the other side is peace and strength.

As I locked the door, I started feeling stronger and less resentful. It is not up to you to feed the world. It is detrimental to give this way. It is unhealthy and just leads to resentment and burnout. Giving when you have something in reserve for yourself is the sweet spot. Giving from your overflow is the best feeling. There are no frustrations associated with it because you aren't starving. You are calm, secure, and satiated. It is easy to be generous with others when you are in a good place yourself.

It's kind of like when you feed wildlife. If you continue to feed the birds or the squirrels, they start to develop a habit or the innate knowledge that the nice lady with the crazy hair puts out peanut butter and seeds. They just have to show up. Instead of wasting time foraging for themselves and finding food on their own as God intended, they'll just swing by Gail's All You Can Eat Seed Buffet! "It's so easy!" They start to get fat and happy off your resources and lose the want or desire to go get some on their own. Over time, this weakens the animals because they lose their natural instincts. By overgiving, you are crippling the other person. You are destroying their motivation and self-sufficiency by allowing them to abuse this unbalanced cycle of give and take.

So, stop feeding the creatures in your life! When your kids can talk, they can start doing things themselves. You can start small and build on the difficulty level as they get older. Your goal should be to raise your children to be healthy, independent people who can take care of themselves. The sooner you start the transfer of responsibility, the less resistance you will have. Anyone who started late with teenagers knows!

People with addictions are the most difficult to stop feeding because they are masters of manipulation and guilt. They know the exact things to say to get you to open those cupboard doors. That is the worst thing you can do, though.

You must fight your pattern of helping that is actually harming and respond with complete consistency. You can tell them, "You are capable and need to stand on your own two feet." You can say, "I hope you find the answer to that," from behind the closed, locked door. They will continue to bang on it and wail and scream until they realize it doesn't work anymore. Eventually, if you are strong enough to ignore their hissy fits, they will concede and walk away to find another way to get what they want. That is why consistency is so important. If you tell them no, but then open the cupboard anyway and give them the cheese, they will come back again and again, remembering that one time their manipulation worked. At that point, you are stuck in this dynamic that much longer. The fastest way to correct this behavior is with complete and total consistency. It is also the most difficult.

Stay strong! Keep the doors shut. Lock 'em up! You deserve to enjoy and feed yourself with the resources you have fought to secure. Don't give it all away.

The Big Takeaway Question: Who am I hurting with my codependent behaviors?

It might be hard for you to see your giving as hurting, but this is an important point to acknowledge. Take an inventory of all your relationships and evaluate for codependency. Make adjustments and set boundaries as appropriate. Lock your cupboard doors.

BOUNDARIES

Healthy people have boundaries. They have a standard of treatment that they require of other people who enter their lives. I did not have any for a very long time. Somewhere between total openness and total lockdown is a healthy place in the Land of Boundaries.

You get to decide what you will accept, and this can change at any time. You dictate whether your kids can drop an F-bomb in front of you, or whether your ex-husband can dump his financial drama in your lap. You decide if your sister can dump her kids at your house and party all weekend, every weekend.

For a very long time I was a go with the flow, keep the peace kind of person, and as a result, I had few boundaries and let a lot of bad behavior slide. As I got healthier in my mind, I knew I had to do something different because people will always meet you at the lowest barrier to entry. If your bar is low, they will do the minimum required to clear it. If your bar is high, they will be required to meet you at least at that level.

I used to wait, thinking people would police themselves,

that eventually, they would do the right thing. Then I would be shocked and stunned that they never did. They always met my minimum requirements. I held myself to a higher standard, but because I didn't hold *them* to a higher standard, life became a frustrating exercise in futility. They would continue their bad behavior, and I would be silently outraged at their audacity.

This was a skill I had to learn late in life, and it was a harder habit to break, mostly because people were used to getting away with murder with me. They rebelled and hated it when I changed, but I tried to be as consistent as possible, and I am happy to say that things are changing.

If you find yourself in a similar place, here is where to start. Get clear. Get really clear on what you want and need. Sometimes, the easiest way to do this is to really go back to what torques you off, what events have happened that made you angry. Oftentimes, a lack of boundaries invites disrespect, and our reaction to disrespect is outrage or anger. Reverse engineering what is irritating you is an easy way to get in touch with what needs to change. You will also need to stop apologizing for having a standard, and don't lower your standard when you have someone rebel against it. That is about them, never you.

Brutal honesty and not stuffing your frustrations are key to holding the new standards you set. Giving feedback immediately and in a loving way is the key to making these changes with the least amount of resentment. Call your feelings what they truly are instead of saying nothing. Tell your son, "It hurt my feelings when you blew me off. I am disappointed in what you did." Tell your draining friend, "I'm going to stop you right there," when they launch into the thousandth conversation about why Sara down the street copies everything they do. "I am not going to participate in this negativity." So what if it hurts their feelings? Self-preservation is key now, and sadly, it will feel like you are being selfish. This will sound the alarms if you are an over-giver, and it will be a skill you need to force yourself to learn. Just embrace it with honesty. If someone who has a problem with your new boundaries is bold enough to call you out on it, be bold enough back to say, "You know what? I am making some positive changes in my life, and setting boundaries is one of those areas, so I am evaluating who and what I want in my life now. What you're doing might have been okay in the past, but it is not okay now."

Not everyone who shows up deserves entrance into your castle. It's time to build a moat and some really high walls you lock down securely with a secret password. Boundaries limit the crazy. They turn away the drama queens and the lopsided takers in your life. They protect your energy and emotions. Boundaries create separateness and allow you to reconnect with your power. That is why it is hard to create boundaries with family and why those closest to you are likely the biggest violators. We crave connection and to be with people so deeply that our boundaries often take a back seat in favor of keeping these people in our lives. All this does is create bigger problems down the road. The most loving relationships are born of trust and respect. Boundaries are the workhorse of these two qualities because they teach people how to behave and how to treat you. They allow you to trust your partners more fully because your boundaries have been respected.

Have you ever been to an outdoor concert venue the morning after, when all the grass is trampled and plastic beer glasses litter the field, cracked and smashed? That is the kind of bad behavior that having no boundaries encourages. People don't follow the rules unless they have to. If you have teenagers, you know their behavior changes based on who is in front of them and what they know about that person's boundaries. They know how to act in front of their hard-ass English teacher or how to get away with murder at Nonna's house. They are incredibly adept at recognizing these invisible boundaries with the people in their lives without being told.

Everyone tests boundaries, especially teenagers. They push to test their strength, to know exactly what they can and cannot do. A strong boundary that has been tested and proven to be secure helps a person feel safe. I know this seems counterintuitive, but it is true. Without boundaries, there is fear and chaos. Boundaries equal safety and love.

I made a lot of mistakes parenting my kids after my divorce. Mostly, I let the boundaries slide because of the guilt I felt about destroying their family. After life had been so difficult for so long, I wanted things to be easy, and at first, it was. But eventually, all it did was condone bad behavior, and I had to make major adjustments.

Teenagers live to push your boundaries, to push their parents' buttons as far as they can. Some kids naturally push harder than others. They are rule-breaking thrill-seekers who need the strongest and biggest boundaries available. They will fight against them with every fiber of their being because they hate to be controlled, but ultimately, these types of kids need them most because they are reckless and immature and will hurt themselves without them. The rule followers are more self-governing. They approach life with more fear and a desire to please. They still need boundaries, but do not need the enforcement as much because they won't be the ones straddling the line, tiptoeing right to the edge. Instead, they will be a few feet inside, just to be safe. Both types of teenagers need them, but one will make it easier on you.

Boundaries are important in romantic relationships, too. They set expectations so there are fewer disappointments.

They give your partner a minimum to adhere to. Being upfront with your boundaries is part of navigating a healthy relationship and helps build trust. It's not a free for all, where you are just incredibly happy to have been chosen. It is a standard that tells the other person, "This is what I need from you to be happy in this relationship." It invites a feeling of safety in the relationship because you understand and agree to the rules.

If you are with a partner who knows your boundaries but violates them time after time, stop wasting your time and get out. That is a man who is disrespecting you, and love cannot coexist with disrespect. There are men out there who *will* work to respect your boundaries. They will be driven to earn your trust. They are not unicorns. They do exist.

The Big Takeaway Question: What are my boundaries?

Journal on your current boundaries. Break them into categories. If you have kids, what are your boundaries with them? In your romantic relationship, what are the boundaries there? The clues of someone crossing a boundary are contained in the fights you have. If the same issue triggers you, what behavior is happening to set off that reaction?

Some examples to get you started: With your children, are they allowed to swear in front of you, or listen to music in front of you with lyrics you don't condone? Are they expected to always pick up your phone calls, or text when they are running late?

With your romantic relationships, are you allowed to raise your voice in anger? Are social media and phone passwords shared? Can you text people of the opposite sex? Can a partner go out with friends of the opposite sex without the other partner present? How frequently are you required to communicate? Is the relationship monogamous?

ENERGY VAMPIRES

It's easy, especially if you are codependent, to get into the bad habit of giving until it hurts. Giving away your energy is so easy and leaves you in a depleted state where eventually you cannot continue, like a car that has run out of gas. Being raised as a good Catholic girl, I was assigned the typical female stereotype of filling the supportive role. The mantra of serving and doing for others was beaten into me day after day until it became something I had to unlearn. This stage of life that I'm in now requires me to ruthlessly edit who comes into my life, who stays in my life, and who gets my energy. Protecting myself from the energy vampires has become of paramount importance to allow me to redirect the energy I am given daily to take care of and heal myself.

The way you can tell if you are in energy debt is that you are exhausted nearly constantly and stay frustrated. You are stressed out over other people's problems more than they are. You are starting to resent being taken advantage of. You are just plain tired and have the symptoms of burnout.

You need to do an energy audit and find out where the holes are, like when you have an energy audit in your house to see where it needs insulation. The same principle applies to your internal energy. Find the energy suckers and eliminate or repair them. This will require you to pull back more and be less helpful to others than you have been in the past. You will need to prepare yourself for backlash. You will need to learn how to say no much more frequently. You will need to silence the guilt that keeps you prisoner, doing things you really don't want to do. You will need another way to identify yourself because your identity might be tied up in this unhealthy role.

What? You aren't going to wash my practice jersey while I play video games anymore? You won't run to fetch me a McChicken on my lunch break? How am I going to eat? It will be easy to get swept into the guilt tornado that comes with protecting your energy. Do not do this. Batten down the hatches and hold your ground. You have to teach the people in your life a new way to treat you. When they voice their objections, you might need to tell them, "In the past, I have engaged in some unhealthy behaviors, so things are going to change, and you are going to need to take a more active role in your own life." They will hate this because that requires them to step up and do the things you were doing for them.

One of the hardest things to do is sit in the no-help zone with someone. To set your boundary firmly and then wait and hold your ground. You will have to learn that it is okay to do nothing instead of rushing around. Let them handle it themselves. With children, this is very difficult, because you might have been told that doing is loving. It will feel nearly excruciating to sit on your hands while you empower them through the use of the word no. You can be a resource. You can be available to talk through solutions and give advice if they want it, but the doing is now their responsibility. Right now, the giver in me is twisting in agony. My son needs to get his wisdom teeth out. He's eighteen now, though, and an adult. An adult takes care of their health. I have sent him all the information he needs to make an appointment. Time will tell if he steps up and does this very basic thing he needs to do, or if he waits until it's an emergency.

Givers get called doormats, something that is walked all over and permanently there for you to wipe your shitty shoes on so you don't ruin the carpet. I hated that word because it made me feel weak. No one wants to be called a doormat. Let that anger fuel your change. Let those who walked over you find their own way to clean their own shitty shoes.

The more you clear the takers in your life that over-burden you with their constant requests, you will then be able to take that energy and do something you love with the overflow. You will be able to focus your mental capacities on finding a new job, making a decision about if it is the right time to buy a new car, or healing from a painful break-up. It takes resources to get yourself to a healthy place, and giving all yours away to people who are too lazy to do their own work does two things. It makes it impossible for you to get to a happy, healthy place, and it deprives them of the growth they need to do personally. You are only allotted so much energy on any given day. Avoid energy debt with healthy boundaries and by encouraging responsibility.

When you finally make the real conscious decision to change, it will be a one step forward, two steps back process. You will slip easily into your old ways. Don't beat yourself up for it, just recognize it is happening and make a new healthier decision. Early on, I found myself having to erase multiple replies in text messages because of my pattern of over-helping. This is normal as you learn new ways to interact. Remember the pause at this stage. There is almost nothing that needs an immediate response. If you can let it go for twenty-four hours, most of these requests will likely disappear.

I am at the point in my life where I am now putting in the same amount of effort that other people give me. If you take and I can never rely on you, then you don't have a place at my table anymore. If you only text when you need something, or you guilt me into doing things I don't want to do, then I choose not to respond to you and that is okay. I let all calls go to voicemail. Instead of interrupting my day with other people's chaos, I respond when it is convenient for me. I protect my mornings like they are sacred. This is the time when I focus on my own goals, and I don't let anything distract me from them anymore. Keeping that promise to myself means I am using the best part of my energy in ways that support the life I want to live. Having more resources for the ones in my life who deserve them and for me to heal myself has changed everything. I have the energy to do the work that needs to be done internally, and as a result, things are getting better in record time.

You were not sent here to be an empty, exhausted, used up sack of skin. You were sent here to become. To become the most beautiful version of you while using your unique gifts in the highest way. This takes energy, so when you give it all away, you are left just half-assing what you were born to be. You are settling in the worst way. You deserve better. Stop giving until it hurts. Stop giving until you are used up and empty. Redirect the love and effort you pour on others to yourself.

The Big Takeaway Question: Who are the energy vampires in your life?

Analyze all the relationships in your life, being brutally honest about the amount of effort you expend. Look for ways to set boundaries, encourage responsibility, or cut energy vampires out completely, guilt-free, to conserve your energy for your own health and healing.

DEAD INSIDE

Around midlife is when people start to wake up and look around. Throughout your twenties and thirties, you have probably been distracted by all sorts of things—men, relationships, jobs, raising kids, and finding your place in the world. If things weren't perfectly peachy, then you probably self-soothed in one or more ways—overeating, drinking, shopping, sex. There are so many ways you can choose to stay occupied enough that you don't have to think too much or too hard about what you really want. It is easy to get to a comfortable place where you settle in for a long winter's nap. Years can go by while you are comfortable enough thinking this must be what happy means.

As your responsibilities mount, you might have to make concessions, trading your hours for dollars in ways that aren't really in line with what makes you happy. That works temporarily. On the treadmill of life, you phone it in, work for the man, and then distract yourself with the shiny things working for the man buys to make the sacrifices more palatable. Over time, the fire in your eyes starts to dwindle, and by the time you hit your forties, your light is on the verge of burning out. You are barely alive, merely existing. The day to day grind of settling has made you dead inside.

When you live your life off-purpose for decades, the disconnect is a slow death. It emaciates you internally and manifests on the outside in addictions, anger, and overeating. Because as a whole you are unhappy, you are searching for that quick fix to change your state of mind, so you reach for the wine or a cupcake. Something that will make you feel better temporarily, and it does, and then you find yourself bottoming out again and reaching for another one. It's an endless cycle of self-punishment.

The only way out is to rekindle the fire within you, to get back in touch with your unique talents and power that only you bring into this world. It is chasing the dream that everyone thinks is a waste of time, when deep inside, you know it is the only thing that has ever made sense.

I met a seventy-seven-year-old man once who was an angry alcoholic. I asked him what he had done for a living, and he told me he was an insurance agent since he had six mouths to feed. Then I asked him what he really wanted to do, and he said he had wanted to be a painter. He was a physical representation of what happens when a person lets their dream die. It's sad to see a whole life wasted on selling insurance when he could have taken a different, more fulfilling path. He had responsibilities, and I get that. I would have encouraged him to keep the internal fires going by continuing to paint on weekends, and to carve some time out of his schedule that was set aside for painting. Inside any life, there are many hours wasted—watching TV, Netflix, and scrolling on social media. If you eliminated just those behaviors, you would earn the time to continue to practice the things that do bring you joy.

So many people could be extras in *The Walking Dead*. Braindead zombies in hordes following the next one off the cliff unless someone puts them out of their misery. It doesn't have to be like this. It does require a commitment to yourself to practice your joy inside your allotted time and responsibilities. There is always time you can steal, and when you start to find the time to do the things that light you up, then more time will magically appear because your joy impacts your energy. Things that light you up *add* energy to your life, not subtract it. If you engage in this practice daily, you miraculously find more time to practice, and your life will begin to light up again. That light can never be extinguished because it comes from deep within.

Don't let life force you so far off course that it makes you dead inside. Make conscious choices and decisions to wake up and reclaim your life. Don't numb out. Face the reality of the life you are living and see if it aligns with the one you want to live. If it doesn't, start taking real steps to bring them into congruence.

The Big Takeaway Question: Are you dead inside?

Are you simply existing? Is each day the same as the one before? Do you want more from the life you are living? Find scraps of time you can carve out for your own pursuit of happiness.

EMPATHS BEWARE

Where my empaths at? It's a beautiful thing to be an empath in a world this cruel, but if you aren't careful, the wrong people will be drawn to you and you will destroy yourself to save them. I'm one of those people who physically can feel pain from others in a room. The kind of person who can go to the funeral of someone I have never met and sob like a baby because of the collective suffering around me. It is incredibly embarrassing.

An empath is an emotional sponge, soaking up everything around them, the good and the bad. This is the reason an empath needs to have boundaries and surround themselves with only healthy people. If you do not, you will suffer, even die inside the prison of relationships you shouldn't be in.

I love that I'm an empath, but years of practice have shown me what I need to do in order to survive as an empath in this world. When, essentially, your heart is on the outside of your body without the protective cage of your ribs. When you feel things more deeply than the average human. I have been in relationships where I have been mocked for this quality, where I have been told to go "feel my feelings." I have been labeled a feelings monster, and although it is accurate, it still stings. But knowing these things about myself and the potential that my empathy can result in pain, I still wouldn't have it any other way.

The empaths of the world bring comfort and love. You read people so intuitively and clearly that it's like you have a sixth sense. You tread lightly around people who are suffering, careful to never be the cause of it. This is a beautiful way to live and must be preserved and protected at all costs.

It's almost like magic, being so in tune with other humans and sometimes even animals. Picking up energies like a tuning fork that only a small percentage of people can actually hear. It is an incredible gift.

My daughter is an empath as well, and I think it is my duty to teach her the ropes of how to keep this quality intact, yet still protect her own heart. When she was a little girl, she loved so hard that even the first few bars of the Sarah McLachlan song on the ASPCA commercial would wreck her for the day. I literally would run to scoop up the remote, sliding across my king-sized bed like in a Jason Statham movie, trying to head off all that pain.

It's important to embrace all of who you are instead of trying to change yourself to fit into what is expected of you. I used to curse my introvert, empath ways. I yearned to be the kind of girl that everyone loved at a party, who was free to mingle confidently instead of nursing a beer in the corner and getting the sweats just from knowing I was going to have to make small talk with strangers. Now, I just don't accept invites to things I don't want to do. Instead of forcing myself to participate in a social event that will require two days of downtime to replenish, I just take smaller bites of interaction. It is not a weakness. It is acknowledging who I am and setting my priorities in line with that. The freedom this kind of thinking gives you is amazing. There is absolutely nothing wrong with anything you want in your life, as long as it doesn't harm yourself or other people. Embrace your inherent qualities. Enjoy the perks of them instead of beating yourself up, wishing you were different. Enjoy your empathy and your intuitiveness that has you able to shake down your kids with a single look.

You should strive to be an empowered empath, an empath with boundaries, a healthy empath. It is much more difficult, but in the end, it is so much healthier. It is the only way an empath can survive and truly be happy. All the other roads lead to your total depletion and eventual destruction.

Empaths are often mislabeled as fragile. That is a lie. An empath is so exceedingly strong, able to dive into painful depths with an innate understanding that most people can't even fathom. Empaths go deep, mining the strongest feelings of the heart. Surface dwellers will never understand this, and that is okay because their strengths lie in other areas. A surface dweller will not understand why an empath would give away that kind of effort and energy to another person, or why they would want to in the first place. An empath will not understand how a surface dweller could stop themselves from doing it. Both personalities are important in the world we live in. Both have their place. My surface dweller partner guards my heart and gently tells me when I am doing too much. He helps me set boundaries.

Empaths can breathe in these deep places of despair and help others navigate to safety. Empathic strength is being able to hold space for someone in pain, accompany them on their journey, and provide gentle support. It is exhausting being an empath, and I think that is why most empaths are introverts. One of the most important skills you will have as an empath is discerning who deserves your empathy and energy. You should always be on the lookout for narcissistic energy types because the pairing of a narcissist and an empath is always a disaster for the empath.

If you are an empath, that is truly a gift. The world needs more people who are deeply in tune with others. Who can see and feel the struggles and the challenges that people face, outside themselves, with emotional clarity. Who can hold space for a person navigating their way through an intensely emotional time with understanding and love. If you are an empath, you are a superhero.

The Big Takeaway Question: How can you practice empathy in a healthy way?

Even if you are not an empath, it is worthwhile to develop this quality. Empathy is quiet and supportive. It doesn't forge ahead for a solution. It doesn't minimize someone's pain by saying, "Well, things could always be worse." It acknowledges the other person's struggle or pain and holds space for a person's emotions. It gives them permission to process them without judgment or solutions. Empathy says, "I have been there. I am here for you."

FEAR OR LOVE

According to Marianne Williamson, who has written some incredibly powerful books on healing and transformation, there are only two emotions: fear and love. I never distilled it down to just two, but when I heard that statement on Oprah's Super Soul Podcast, it resonated so deep, all the way down to my bones, that I knew it was true. I began to look at my days differently, classifying them as a day spent in fear or love, and it was easy to see that the fear days vastly outnumbered the love days.

How much of your life is spent in the fear zone? Fear is tightness. It constricts, it shatters everything, and it depletes. Your body chemistry changes. Your hormones and your bones change. Being in the fight or flight mode for too long burns you out and taxes you emotionally and physically. All the negative emotions can be traced back and originated from fear. Anger, jealousy, the need to control, disgust, contempt, hatred, anxiety, and depression—all of these are rooted in fear. The fear of not being enough, worthy enough, loving yourself enough to step out into love. Men express anger easier than fear because it is socially acceptable for them to be angry instead of scared.

Love is expansive and inclusive. It forgives and is accepting. The hardest thing to do is to love people who wrong you or take advantage of you, but this is the clearest path to happiness. Love is light and ease and flow. It is laughter, uncontrolled and bubbling up. It is security and strength. Love is allowing. It is trusting the other person to live their life and knowing that you will be okay no matter what. It is cutting the dependence on the outcome of someone else's decisions to make you happy.

Sitting in fear is the path to hell on earth. Fear comes from anxiety driven by past punishing or forward thinking. Most of my life was spent in this never-ending chess game of trying to see around the corners and preemptively strike. Half of the stuff in your mind that you are crunching out solutions for won't even happen. Look at all that brain power you've wasted. All that time and effort. Repurpose that energy into something worthwhile. It's hard to retrain your brain to do that, almost like a mediation practice. See that you are doing it, bring your focus back to center and back to the present, and then let go of your need to control. Let go of the fear of the outcome and step into love.

For people who like to control, the type A personalities who sweat without a schedule, it will be difficult to learn to let go and allow. I know this is true because I used to be that person. My mind would spin and spin, whipping up solutions for everyone—my ex-husband, my kids, my business, my life. I was completely absorbed in this chess game that I was playing that never worked out the way I plotted it because other people made different decisions. I would try to guilt them or shame them into following my perfect plan, but all that did was breed frustration and rebellion in the ones I loved most. My controlling ways got me nowhere but exhausted. It was hard to let go and trust that they could make the right decision on their own. When I saw them suffering from the consequences that could have been avoided if only they would have listened to me. When I read that, I see the asshole that I was, the smug controlling asshole that was too far up in everyone else's business.

Control is a waste. It never works. The reason so many of you get stuck in the control cycle is that it seems like it is working, to an extent. When, in reality, all it does is create a divide between you and the people you are trying to control. You may relabel it as helping. You may tell yourself, "I am just trying to save people time, and I know best." A lot of people, mothers, in particular, think control is love. This is just a way to rationalize control, so you feel that it is okay to continue. The reality is that you cannot control anyone else in your life. You can only control yourself and your own behavior. Control is based on fear, too, because it says, "I am afraid to let you make your own decision because I am afraid that it will not line up with what I want and need." It says, "You have to do this my way because I am afraid of what will happen if you don't." So, I had to learn to stay in my own lane. To only work to control and guide my own life.

Love is allowing them to make decisions and then being there to encourage them when they hit a painful consequence, or celebrating when they have a win. Love is relaxing into life and letting go of the steering wheel instead of white-knuckling it with your shoulders hunched, bracing for impact. It is letting them drive instead of always grabbing the keys out of their hand. It is being available if they want advice, shutting up if they don't, and cheering them on to do what is right for them. It is swallowing the I told you so comments, letting the person make mistakes, and forgiving them when they do.

Every day is a choice. Do you want to live in love today or

fear? Every person you interact with, you get to make another decision. Will you respond to them with love or fear? I am writing this book a month after the George Floyd murder at the hands of law enforcement. Nothing drives this point further home than this event and the riots that followed. It is the summer of fear. The pandemic is at record highs, and in Iowa, kids are mandated by the governor to return to schools while the cases are soaring. People are scared and anxious. Fear makes people do destructive things. When law enforcement went down on their knees in front of protestors, the fear subsided. The riots became calmer. The protestors' voices could be heard, and things started to change. There is a long way to go. The loss of George Floyd shined a spotlight on a lack of love that has been missing for centuries. The only cure right now for our broken world is love. The only cure is understanding each other better and moving away from fear into love.

The Big Takeaway Question: Are you living in fear or love?

Look back at the last week or the last month. How much of your life was lived in fear? How much was lived in love? What emotions does fear bring up for you? What emotions does love bring up for you? Then, in the following week, when you feel the fear come to the surface in whatever flavor you choose, acknowledge this. Take a deep breath and try to reframe what is happening into love, acceptance, and allowing. You don't have to love it when shitty things are happening. You do need to accept it, though, and look for the seed of good in it. There always is one.

DECISION SPINNING

Decision-making can be your biggest strength or your greatest weakness. Because I didn't focus on the right things after my divorce, I was steeped in fear of wasting time or making another mistake that would cost me another twenty years. I met and went out with great guys and not so great guys. I was engaged twice to the same man and broke up with him twice.

I was waking up at 2, 3, and 4 am regularly, and immediately, my mind spin would begin consuming nearly all my effort and attention. I found myself spending 90% of my awake time questioning the relationship, what I wanted, and if this was the right guy. This went on and on during two separate occasions for several months. That should have been a red flag for sure, but at the time, it was barely pink. I thought there was something wrong with me, something that didn't work right, that I had some internal flaw which meant I would never be happy.

Instead of having the resources to focus on work, or healing myself, or dealing with the incredibly heavy problems that come with raising two clinically depressed teenagers, all of my resources were exhausted by this indecision. I realized later that not making a decision *is* a decision. It is choosing to stay stuck and not move forward. It is fear that holds you back, but it also forces you into this exhausting space warp time suck that goes nowhere.

People always say, "I want to move forward. I want to move forward." Decision spinning is not the way. Instead of moving forward, you remain incredibly busy, yet go nowhere. Instead of a straight-ish line headed toward your happiness, it is a squiggly line that circles the same spot over and over like a dog trying to find the perfect place to poop.

Your brain is a fixed resource, and you truly only have a certain amount of energy each day. It is better to make a decision and put a clock on it. I will give this relationship six months. I will show up and do my best, and then reevaluate after six months whether I should stay or go. I will be single until my birthday. I will give this new job one year to settle in, and then decide if it aligns with my future. Make the decision and then let it go. Free your mind to focus on something else, something more important than going over and over the pros and cons of the decisions that are weighing on you right now.

I used to think everything was so deeply connected. I used to believe the butterfly theory was real. This is simply not the case. You make a decision, and then the universe morphs into the next scene. It is constantly changing to line up with the path you are taking like a never-ending "choose your own adventure" book. There is no right decision, and there is no wrong one. Whatever path you choose is the right one. Everything is not as deeply connected as I once thought. It is not a life or death battle. It is simply a path. Once you decide which one to take, another one will open up, and you will have to make another decision. It's like when you go on a spontaneous road trip, nearly anyplace you go can be beautiful if you choose to see the beauty. You can't go wrong. Iowa is gorgeous, but so are South Dakota and Colorado and Florida.

The fear of making the wrong decision is a paralyzing place to be. I know, because I lived there for nearly three years. All that time and effort wasted, and for what? During that time, I depleted myself completely and never got one step closer to any of my goals. Once I finally learned what I was doing to myself, I almost wanted to cry for the self-inflicted pain and unease I subjected myself to for so long. This one lesson freed me in many ways, but most importantly, it freed my mental energy to focus on other things, the things I truly wanted. The things I was born to create.

Part of the reason you can't make a decision is that you don't trust yourself. You don't think you can evaluate the options and make a good decision. You've been hurt so much in the past, so you are gun shy. I've been there. I get you! But you are smarter and stronger than you realize. To be an adult in this world, you have to have survived some pretty difficult things. No one gets to middle-age unscathed. You have proven you can survive and overcome challenges. Why can't you trust in your ability to take what is coming next in stride, to be able to handle whatever will come your way?

Set down the fear, anxiety, and worry. Do this by refocusing your thoughts on goodness. Even in the midst of truly terrible events, there is always some tiny nugget you can be thankful for. Gratitude is a positive and creative emotion that chokes the fear and anger out. It is impossible to be grateful and hateful at the same time. They simply cannot co-exist. Hate, fear, worry, and anxiety are heavy on your back, and none of them are useful in your journey of life anyway. They don't feed you or sustain you in any way. Travel lighter through life, enjoying more of the scenery, without the weight of these toxic emotions, and know that you can change it up anytime you want.

Sometimes, you have been trained by other people not to make decisions in the first place. This is detrimental because it takes you down someone else's road. When you put your life and future in their hands and refuse to participate in the decision-making process, you weaken yourself. Someday, you will wake up so far away from your destination and have to make sweeping changes to realign with what you want. Never let anyone have that kind of power in your life.

Sometimes, you give a decision more power than you should. You blow it out of proportion in your mind and think your whole life hinges on this one moment. It does not. Very few decisions are that powerful. Your emotions can magnify the wrong things and distort the stakes. Emotions are incredibly powerful. They can warp reality and blow events and interactions up in your mind. If you are an emotional person as opposed to a logical person, part of your journey will be learning how to disconnect the feelings in order to make appropriate choices. Hindsight will also try to reinforce this idea of right vs. wrong. Do not buy into this lie.

When I look back on the last few years, specifically the decision we made to move to Des Moines, I could clearly blame it as being wrong for my son. But the reality is that he had the DNA of addiction, and that is not location dependent. It would have found him anyway. When I finally accepted this truth, it set me free from the guilt I felt about the decision I made.

Life unfolds the way it was meant to, regardless of the decisions you make. If you can put your trust in that truth, then it becomes easier to set aside the agony, the worry, and the struggle. If you can look at it more lightly, you will find the best path to take. You are smart, and you *can* trust yourself.

One final thing to avoid. I used to pride myself in being able to see ten steps ahead and finding the trolls under the bridges. This was an even bigger waste of my time and energy because, most of the time, the scenarios never materialized. I was so good at looking for potential problems and pre-engineering solutions that my mind worked overtime. I pre-worried about nearly everything. Talk about an energy suck. No wonder the Buddha is always blabbing about the present. I finally figured out that he is on to something there.

Make a decision. Let it go. Make another one. Let it go. It gets easier with practice. I promise.

The Big Takeaway Question: What decisions are you spinning out on?

Write down all the decisions you are currently trying to make. Pick one, the easiest one on the list. Make sure you start small, so you can build momentum. Decide what to do, make your decision, and put a clock on it. Take action before you can backslide or think about it more. Once the decision is made, let it go.

In a few days or a week, check in with yourself. How do you feel? Did the world end, or did your path get a little clearer? Return to this list in a week. Pick the next easiest thing. Repeat. Continue with bigger and farther-reaching decisions. Don't waffle back and forth. Decide and move forward to the next one.

THE WAITING PLACE

Dr. Suess was onto something. The waiting place, a place where nothing is happening but anxiety. Where patience is thin and will is weak. It's a place you will find yourself in life a time or two. When I was younger, I sat in there, wringing my hands in anxiety. I got up and paced. I pulled down on my face with my fingers, popping my eyes out in frustration. I was not a good waiter. I was a do-er. It was nearly impossible to calm my mind that was focused on forcing the puzzle pieces of what I thought was best for me together. Waiting was lame. I was ambitious and a go-getter. I ain't got time for that. Life laughed at me and sent me some hard lessons.

The waiting place is a giant lesson in patience and allowing. The waiting place is dark and gloomy. You only get to see one step forward, and that is sometimes covered in fog. You will flail around, trying to get your bearings and trying not to misstep. It will scare the shit out of you. It's easy to have a crappy attitude in the waiting place while letting the worries and anxieties consume you. That is not the way out. It is easy to be jealous and to think that everyone around you is living with more ease and opportunity than you have been given. This is not the way, either. The best way is to joyfully wait. Even if all you can be happy about right now is that your dog still loves to snuggle with you, or the sunrise was pretty, that is enough. You have to protect your mind fiercely when you are in the waiting place. It is too easy to let momentum drag you down and for your mind to play tricks on you by convincing you that things will never get better or that you are doomed.

Focusing on being grateful and positive in the waiting place will make your mind stronger, and the people that are forced to be around you will appreciate you not being a buzzkill all the time. No one likes this part. Universally, it sucks, but if you can find the tiniest bit of joy in the suck-age, then that is enough. That is all you need to sustain you during this time period.

The waiting place also forces you to be open. You can have a plan and try to execute that plan, but an even better plan might be trying to show up for you. Your job is to take action, but temper that action with openness. Don't buckle down and make decisions out of fear and constrict everything in the scary recesses of your mind. When you are stressed, you have tunnel vision. The perfect solution might be cueing up for you, and yet you will not see it because the stress crowds it out. Force yourself to stay open and be patient and wait for what really feels right. This takes immense discipline, especially if you are a type-A personality like me, and not having the next five years of your life planned out gives you the shakes. It is hard to let go of your want to control the outcome and the future. But hey, the truth is you can't control the future anyway, and it's a drain on your resources to white-knuckle this part thinking you can. It's a farce. You control nothing except your response.

You cannot fast forward the waiting place. It will take as

long as it needs to take. The biggest lesson I learned on this was during a particularly punishing time in my life I like to refer to as Sweet Hell Alabama. In 2009, we decided to relocate for warmer weather, put an offer on a house, and it was accepted. Then there was a massive recession and an economic downturn we were not ready for. We had two mortgages—*for five fucking years*. We lost a hundred thousand dollars and ended up coming back to Iowa with our tails between our legs. That period of my timeline was so dark and depressing, I have no idea how I survived. We were stuck in the waiting place that had become more like an insane asylum, and I am ashamed to admit that I was a terrible waiter. I was bitter, angry, and frustrated, and I took it out in unhealthy ways, so it likely took longer to resolve. It was a painful lesson that left many deep scars, but it drove the point home that the waiting place can be as painful as you decide to make it. You can believe that things are coming together for you, or you can wail that they never will. The time will pass regardless.

The good news is that, eventually, your name will get called and you will get to leave the waiting place. The day we sold the Alabama house, I felt like I had been released from prison. I literally danced with my kids in the living room of our house. The freedom tasted so sweet. Looking back now, I see that time as wasted time. I could have focused on any great number of things that would have helped ease the anxiety. I was just too stubborn to do it. Don't be like me!

When your time in the waiting place comes, go there willingly and learn to wait patiently. Learn to trust the process instead of trying to control the outcome. A better outcome that you may have never considered might be trying to come into fruition, but your desire to control might be blocking it. Be open enough for it to be revealed. Wait with hope. Every day in the waiting place is a chance to harness your ability to cultivate happiness in your mind, no matter the circumstance. The choice is whether you allow the waiting place to change you for the better or to make you bitter. Let it make you better.

The Big Takeaway Question: What is your attitude in the waiting place?

Look back over your life and study times when you've been put in the waiting place. When you've had one plan, but life has put the brakes on you. What did you learn? What was your mindset while you waited? How can you approach your next time in the waiting place with more ease and hope?

PEOPLE DON'T CHANGE, BUT YOU CAN

For the most part, people don't change. Change is hard and requires a focused effort that most people can't or won't put in. People who change their lives are in the minority. Most people get up and do the same thing for seventy years and call it a life. When pain rears its ugly head, they distract themselves with the endless buffering buffet. Things like Netflix, food, and even sex that seem to just use up your life but never propel you forward into the life you desire. Change *can* happen, but it is a process that requires constant mindfulness and dedication.

I used to weigh almost 200 pounds. Many people don't know that about me because I have kept it off for six years. My choice from the buffering buffet was always food, especially sugar. Sugar was my source of comfort, my security blanket, and my mood changer. If life gave me lemons, I made a cheesecake with lemon curd and then ate the whole thing with a spoon while watching Netflix. If something awesome happened, I always went out for food or drinks to celebrate. I was a binger. If I started the day off with cake for breakfast, then my mindset shifted to, "I'll start tomorrow. I already ruined it, so I might as well eat all the bad things. How about some chips and salsa? Then I'll wash it down with a margarita and finish it with salted caramels." Eating was always a temporary high that faded almost immediately, and then the shame set in of what I had done. I didn't ever purge, but I could understand why people did it. I understand the internal fight for control in one area of your life when everything else seems out of control.

Now, when I see people who are overweight, I just see pain—pain they are trying to ignore. I feel compassion for them because I have been there myself. I get it. When you are fat, everyone gets to see your pain because it is physically manifested in your body. You can't hide it like other addictions. You walk around in it every day. No one wants to be overweight and unhealthy. I never make fat jokes or try to shame people who struggle with weight because I intimately understand using food as a coping mechanism. I understand how easy it is to put the weight on and how painful and hard it is to take the weight off.

As young as fourteen, I remember being in Woolworth's, a drug store in the mall, and I vividly remember buying diet pills, naively buying into the promises on the box to feel full all day. I remember shopping for a swimsuit and buying one just a little tighter so I would be compelled to lose a little weight to look perfect in it. It was starting that young, an emptiness I needed to fill, that I filled with cupcakes and candy bars. When I think about the girl I was, I want to hug her and tell her how beautiful she is and slap the diet pills out of her hand. I want to fill her up with worthiness and self-esteem, so she doesn't reach for those in the first place.

One day in my late thirties, I got up and I was just sick of it, sick of being tired all the time, sick of feeling invisible, sick of being uncomfortable, and ashamed about the way I looked. So, I got on the elliptical that day and started exercising. It's just thirty minutes. I told myself I could focus on myself for thirty minutes. After about a week of that, I downloaded a food tracker app, and over the course of nine months, I lost sixty-five pounds and got into a single-digit size. Seeing some initial success was enough momentum to propel me forward to continue even when it was hard. I weighed myself every day, and I am ashamed to admit that when I lost weight, I had a great day, everything was awesome, and life was good. On days I didn't lose or, even worse, instead gained, my day was a struggle. I'd be in a bad mood, questioning why I was doing this in the first place. I was the person who was so wrapped up in losing weight that I'd do a second weigh-in after I pooped. How sick is that? Seeing how much the scale affected my day to day happiness pointed out another flaw I needed to work on: being happy no matter what that number said. I stopped weighing myself every day.

When it became noticeable, people would say "You look great! What is your secret?" Just like I did, they were looking for a shortcut, a magic pill to take to fix the problem. But I discovered there aren't any shortcuts. Eat the right stuff and exercise more, preferably with an activity that you love to do, and you will lose weight. As the weight came off, everything felt lighter. I was physically lighter, my mind was clearer, and I was more motivated to start cleaning up the other messes in my life. This led me to the place of knowing that my marriage wasn't healthy for me and I couldn't continue. That truth was the hardest one I ever had to face because it meant destroying my family to save myself.

I wasted a lot of time and effort on trying to change others. Looking back, I hate how much energy I wasted on that fool's errand. The only person you can change is yourself. You can look at what is not working in your life and take the steps to change it. That is why you cannot save an addict with love or by controlling their access to a substance. They have to want to change. They have to want to do the work. They can say they want to change, but that is not enough. It takes powerful action to enact real lasting change. It is fucking hard to change, and that is why people relapse. That is why people gain the weight right back, and then some. That is why lottery winners lose all their money. Your life has a homeostasis point on nearly everything, a point of maintenance that it settles at, and the only way to change that point is by constant effort, creating new habits, and finding healthier behaviors to replace the old unhealthy ones.

When your life is not working out, you might have a laundry list of things you want to change. Pick one change you want to make and work on that for the next sixty days. It's easy to say "I want to lose weight and exercise and stop smoking and save half my income." If you try to undertake all of these at the same time, you are destined for failure. The overwhelm will revert you back to your homeostasis point in mere hours. It takes a long time to develop an unhealthy habit. It took me nearly a decade to put on all that extra weight, so I had to learn to be patient when it was taking longer than I wanted to come off.

Don't multitask when you are trying to make life changes. It will take all of your life force to make one real sustainable change. Focus all your energy on that one thing. Once you have made progress over a sixty-day time period, then think about the next thing you want to tackle and take on that task for the next sixty days. Over a year's time, you will see such progress that it will encourage you to take on bigger self-improvement projects.

You can change. At any point in your life, you can wake up one day and say, "I am so fucking sick of this. This cannot continue." You can make a plan for yourself and put in the work it takes. You are strong. You are worthy. You deserve to live a life that fits you and makes you proud and happy.

The Big Takeaway Question: What changes do you want to make?

Make a list of the changes you want to make. Don't get overwhelmed by this list, just pick one and start there. Focus all your effort on that one thing for the entire next sixty days. Every day, take one step closer to supporting this new habit or way of life you want to live. Little steps add up to big results. Do not tackle more than one change at a time.

WHO GIVES A SHIT WHAT OTHER PEOPLE THINK?

Me. I gave a shit. For a really long time. And then I learned not to give a shit, and it completely freed me. Looking back now, I am shocked at the amount of time I spent worrying about other people, what they thought, if they liked me, or if they were talking about me behind my back. Next was Olympic level people pleasing, to make sure people liked me and spoke well of me. I wasted so much time in the land of worry about what other people thought.

The truth is, they weren't thinking about me at all. I was obsessing over what they were thinking about *me*, and they were thinking about *themselves*—their homework, their job, their weekend plans. Occasionally, their focus might flit over to me, if I became part of their immediate experience, but then it would settle right back to themselves. Yet I sat in anxiety and hand-wringing worry that they were mad at me if they were too quiet or didn't return a phone call.

This is a natural way to think as a teenager, when your focus is pulled away from your family unit and then thrust out into the world of popularity contests and fitting in. This is the way of the world when you are sixteen. Sitting in anxiety about the way you look, the way you dress, the car you drive. All of these things are external and stupid, but at the time, they all seem so important. The problem becomes when you don't recognize this behavior and let go of it in adulthood, when you continue this cycle. It can be a very crippling and exhausting way to live, toiling away for the approval of other people.

My daughter is fifteen and has the craziest, most fearless sense of style in a person I have ever met. She decided one day she wanted to shave her head, literally down to the skin, which I thought was a nearly criminal act, because she has always had the most beautiful, thick, strawberry blonde hair and an amazing hairline. It was May, school was getting out for the summer, and she was dying to shave her head. She begged and begged, and I eventually relented after much pleading and begging. After all, it's her head, and it's just hair, so why not? I gave her the green light to do it on the last day of school because I knew the act would cause a ruckus at her suburban, overprivileged school. Where the high school parking lot is full of beamers and Audis that parents have bought for their children, and where the latest iPhone is in nearly every hand.

The day came, and she was so excited. She walked into my bathroom, pulled out the electric clippers, and started in, and I was shaking while recording the whole thing. Long blonde waves drifted down like snow, landing on the cold tile floor. She was beaming. Completely in control, her hand was sure and steady, and she kept saying, "I love it!" After twenty minutes, she had no hair on her head longer than a quarter of an inch. She was glowing. Freedom personified, she ran to her room to start a theatrical makeup application and find the right accessories to accent her new look. While I shut the door to my bedroom, swept the hair into a neat pile with my fingers, and threw it into the garbage, tears started to fill my eyes. I stayed hidden until I could control my emotions because I didn't want her to see that discarding her gorgeous hair in a fuck you to femininity act was painful for my traditionally-minded mommy heart.

The next day, I drove her to school, and seeing the usual groups of girls congregating in packs in front of the school, my stomach dropped. Forcing cheerfulness into my voice, I said, "You look great! Go rock it!" She opened the car door and started bravely walking to the entrance of the school. I couldn't drive away. I froze in fear, watching as she walked in, head held high, powerful as hell, and I noticed the head swings and open-mouthed stares. I observed one girl hit her friend with the back of her hand and point at my daughter, and at that moment, I was terrified for her. I whispered a silent prayer, thanking God she only had one day to endure this scrutiny and then she could come home and hide.

When I went to pick her up, I tentatively asked how she was, certain that her whole day had been wrecked by stares and mean girls talking about her. I was ready to hit the ice cream shop for medicinal cones and sitting in the gazebo in the town square to regale her with my sage advice. To my shock and delight, there was none of that. She loved it. She rocked it, and she owned the last day of school in seventh grade. I was in awe. She has such bold confidence at such a young age. I have no idea where she got it from, but I learn more from her every day.

The Big Takeaway Question: Do you find yourself consumed with what people think?

List ways you have sacrificed what you want for the

approval of other people. Have you worried about what people would say about your life, your kids, your relationships, or your career? Set yourself free. The only person whose opinions matter is you.

YOUR ANXIETY IS A LIAR

I've had anxiety as long as I can remember. As a child, it was like my twin, a part of me I couldn't deny that followed me everywhere. Anxiety is a learned behavior developed in childhood. Some kids are natural worriers. If anxiety is unleashed in their lives through childhood trauma, they will become champion level worriers almost instantaneously. The worry will feed the anxiety, and it will be hard to see where one ends and the other begins. It was something that I unknowingly passed on to both of my children. I say unknowingly because, in the eighties, you didn't go to the doctor for mental health issues unless you were getting out the razor blades or hearing voices. Even then, there was such a stigma and denial that mental health was largely ignored in favor of the stiff upper lip. I was raised in the "quit crying or I will give you something to cry about" generation.

Anxiety lied to me constantly. It told me I was stupid, fat, and ugly. It screamed that no one liked me all through high school, when it was so important to be liked. Even in my happiest moments, it said, "You better enjoy this because it won't last forever. You won't be anything. You have nothing to say. Everyone is watching and waiting for you fuck it up. This plane will crash. You'll never find anyone who loves you. You never make good decisions. You are not good enough." Anxiety was a voice that taunted me nearly constantly, a very cunning liar that knew my hot buttons so intimately and didn't hesitate to push them.

Anxiety is lies, lies, lies that you might believe are truths because they come from within you, rooted in childhood worries and your genetic makeup. As a child, I vividly remember my dad getting laid off with seven mouths to feed. I remember my mom getting bags of trash from the neighbor that she painstakingly sorted through in our basement, searching for UPC codes so she could send in a rebate and receive less than a dollar back. The smell of that trash—sour, wet, and moldy cardboard—is seared into my psyche forever. I remember the government cheese and powdered milk and the summer that we ate bratwurst almost every day because it was cheap. The anxiety wonder twins activated in those moments and went hardcore with the internal dialogue. *There is never enough to go around. Money is tough to come by. I have to get mine or I might miss out. I can't afford that.*

I was a professional level worrier. So, as an adult, when the bottom dropped out of my career, I was sent right back to that anxious place in my head, where the lies were on repeat and nearly impossible to silence. The reality was that I have never gone hungry, nor my kids. There has always been a roof over my head and clothing on my body, and the rest is just frosting. After getting laid off, my mind cued up on repeat. "What if you can't pay your mortgage? What if your new business venture never takes off? What if you pour everything into a project and nothing happens?"

Anxiety's bestie is fear. Fear robs all the joy from life, making you overly cautious and incapable of feeling the full depth of joy. You play it safe, wading at the shore in the ocean because you fear the unlikely shark attack, when you really want to let go and let the surf wash completely over your body. Fear steals these moments from you, letting you have a taste of what you want, when you really crave the whole pie.

Anxiety keeps your mind active. Actually, overactive is more accurate, spinning out and stressing out on everything and anything. The only way to quiet your anxiety is to quiet your mind and retrain your internal thought process. You need to re-write your anxious thoughts into calming ones and then repeat them in moments of panic.

My favorite re-engineered thought is, "Everything always works out for me. I'm happy. I'm healthy. I'm wealthy. I'm free." In this phrase, I put the order of importance that I place on these elements in my life. First, I want joy, then health, then money, which together earns my freedom, and it rhymes, which makes it easy to repeat when the stress bunnies dart out. I literally chant this over and over in my mind, and it centers me and brings me back into my own power. This phrase is a simple touchstone I rely on in moments of weakness because, even after years and years of making improvements, I backslide. Under moments of stress, I can slide back into anxiety like it's my job. My brain is a ninja-level worrier, cranking up the stress jack in the box with its creepy carney music and never-ending jump scares. This phrase is a ritual I use to find my center again and again. If you have never tried this, it might sound stupid. You might feel like an idiot. Do it anyway.

The Big Takeaway Question: What anxieties are you harboring?

What thoughts are on repeat in your head? What worries

resurface time after time? When you are under stress, where does your mind go immediately? What stories do you tell yourself about what doesn't work in your life? Re-engineer those thoughts into your new kick-ass mantras. Say them over and over and over, any time anxiety rears its ugly head.

SURVIVOR

Survival comes down to the ability to keep going no matter what has happened. When you are going through something traumatic in nature, survival sometimes looks like not taking a shower, ordering take-out, and eating raw cookie dough from the tube. That is enough, and that is okay. Some days, you will be able to take more on and book yourself an appointment at the therapist, make the hard decision, or make a drastic change in your life, and that is good, too.

The key is to know that everything is coming together in a way that will serve the greater good in the end. That you will find happiness again, no matter how elusive it is right now. Even if the love of your life disappeared, there will be more first kisses and more butterfly-filled first dates if you can only let yourself find the tiniest bit of hope that it is coming. Trust the process and know that it might not be fast, but it will be right. Take comfort in the fact that bad events don't last forever, and neither do the good, and then take a breath and continue.

It helps to look back at your survival moments. I made a

list of mine since I am an avid list maker. It helps to take stock and see that your track record of surviving difficult moments in your life so far is 100%.

I have survived:

- Mother dying from pancreatic cancer
- Getting audited by the IRS
- My own cancer scare and a biopsy
- 2 cross-country moves and losing over 6 figures because of it
- Divorce
- Being cheated on
- Failure of 3 businesses
- Son's overdose
- 5 years of double mortgages
- 2 broken engagements
- 2 emotionally abusive addicts
- Business partners who took advantage of my skills
- Unemployment at 43 with no real degree to fall back on

Don't make the mistake of avoiding the pain. You have to feel it to heal from it. You have to walk through it and get to the other side. You can't numb out and self-soothe with drugs, alcohol, shopping, food, or revenge sex. You have to sit in the pain. Cry and scream to release its physical hold on your body. Burying it deeper and ignoring it will only allow it to fester, to build its strength so it can come surging back into your life, this time with greater consequences. It's easy to temporarily avoid pain in this way, but don't indulge yourself in this behavior.

One of the best ways I have found to deal with pain is to walk it out. When my mom was dying of cancer, I walked and I sobbed. I had to stuff paper towels up my sleeves because the onslaught of tears was so heavy tissues deteriorated. I walked and I talked to God and I verbalized the pain. I blubbered and I sobbed and I screamed. I walked through the pain day after day. Tear after tear, I processed the agony in a healthy way, and I truly think those walks saved me. And later on, when I went to Scotland, the solo walk I had in the bird sanctuary at Aviemore, was where I processed another round of survival pain. When I walked out of that forest, the peace I felt having walked through that pain filled my soul in a way that was so beautiful it brings me to happy tears right now thinking about it.

Finding the smallest amount of joy is the key to surviving anything. When I am in survival mode, which normally comes to me with terrible insomnia, I have found the easiest way to fall asleep is to count my blessings instead of sheep. When life has served up a nice big poop sandwich, it can be really, really difficult to be grateful, but I always start with my kids. I look for one tiny detail about them that I can appreciate. Then I spiral out to my boyfriend, who is continually doing things for me to make life easier. The home I get to live in is warm and safe, and the location is perfect and easy. As you focus on the smallest number of good things, there will be a shift. It may be very small or it could be big, but it is what peace feels like. It could be as small as the dog plopping down next to me to keep me warm while I write, or the fact that my son and I haven't had an explosive event for weeks. These small things will help you focus on the positive and help you survive.

You must also avoid guilt in survival mode. Survival mode is hard enough without the need to compare your life or your reactions to someone else's. If you only get showered today and were only able to hit Chik-fil-A for the kids, that is enough. Don't let guilt and what you should be doing weigh you down and make it even harder to survive. When you are in survival mode, it is time to batten down the hatches and just get through the next period of time. This won't last forever, no matter how much it feels like it will. You will survive this, and someday, it will just be one more thing you get to add to the long list of things you've survived.

Always remember, you are a survivor, you are a warrior, you are strong and capable, and this will be over soon.

The Big Takeaway Question: What have you survived? What can you be grateful for right now?

Make your list of things you have overcome. It will build your confidence that you will triumph over your current challenges. Looking for the things you can be grateful for is the perfect way to realign your mind, which can be manic and messy in survival mode. Finding little pockets of gratitude can get you through your darkest days.

OVERTHINKING & OVERREACTING: NO FUN FOR ANYONE

Overthinking and overreacting are two of the biggest time wasters ever practiced. Spinning your wheels, stuck in the place of considering things to death is where opportunities go to die. Sometimes, you just have to step out in faith, take a chance, and trust that things will work out. Riddling out every foreseeable possible problem and hiccup is a mind-numbing drain of your internal resources because these scenarios rarely ever actually happen. Instead of using your big beautiful brain to create joy and peace in your life, you are crunching it hard to create lack, stress, and worry. The truth is that what you focus on, you create, so turn that genius powerhouse toward something more positive.

I was the queen of overreacting when raising my son. He was a very difficult teenager to parent. I thought my strict Catholic upbringing would come in handy and sort the problem out fast. I thought I could force him to bend to my will, but he was not built like that. All it did was create an atmosphere of distrust. It created an environment where he could never come to me with anything bad because he knew

I would lose it and lock down his life. The sad part is that, when a child feels they can't talk to a parent about something difficult, then they also stop coming to talk about the good things, and the bond between a parent and their child is broken. Here's the thing: teenagers screw up, and the world is vastly different than it was when you were a kid. The technology, the pressure, the possible addictions, and the mental illness these kids are dealing with is night and day compared to the world you grew up in.

If I could go back in time, I would have softened my approach and been more open. I would have stopped reminding him how much he was messing up because that doesn't help. Most people, myself included, could give you a laundry list of their personal flaws right now if you asked them. Believe me, people know when they screw up. They know what their flaws are. They know what they need to change. They don't need you to constantly remind them because it is never very far from their mind.

What I would do, though, is stop saving them and require them to figure it out themselves. Ask questions like, "So, what are you going to do about that?" or "I look forward to hearing your solutions." The lecturing doesn't work, and grounding doesn't work. The only thing that made a difference was tying the current behaviors to creating bigger problems in the future he wanted to live. Even then, we struggled to understand each other, because teenagers are very now-focused, and boys especially have a hard time looking further down the road.

When something traumatic happens, take a time out and don't decide anything for a day, or a few days if it is a major event. You need to give yourself some time to calm down and unwind from the immediate stress of the moment. Making a decision on anything in that heightened state will not do any good. Take some time. Tell the person, "I need some time to process what has happened, so I don't say anything I don't mean. We will talk about it later." Nothing good will come from a decision made in chaos when emotions are running high. Taking the time ensures that you mean what you say, which is important in any relationship, whether it is with kids, a spouse, or friends.

You can literally burn your entire life up by overthinking and then overreacting and then overthinking about the overreacting. I know because I did it. Over time, all that does is deplete your entire system. It destroys you from the inside out, spikes your cortisol levels, and consumes your brain completely so that even things you used to enjoy don't have the same zing because you don't have the energy to enjoy them. Learning the art of non-reaction can be challenging, especially when parenting. Worst case scenario thinking will only ratchet up the stress and anxiety and make everything worse for everyone. The real power is in the pause, to take a step back from the drama and calm your mind. A calm mind can make good decisions, while a stressed brain can develop tunnel vision and will search out a solution that is usually not the healthiest. Stress cuts your brain capacity in half and kicks you into survival mode where only critical processes get the energy, not the deep thinking processes that will bring you to the most elegant solution.

Overthinking is a mind draining exercise that is protective in nature. You are trying to see all the potential problems that might come up and engineering solutions for them before they arise. You might read into things and create stories that you tell yourself in your mind based on false perceptions that can make you spin out and ruin even the good parts of life. Living with anxiety is brutal. I know that first hand. An anxious brain is busy and unfocused, spinning and spinning. It distracts you from being fully present because anxiety is taking up space in your brain, like when you try to listen and comprehend two people speaking at the same time. Or when someone wants to have a conversation during your favorite show, you cannot be fully present for either, so you end up losing half of both of them. You get the gist and that is it. The gist is not enough.

To stop this way of living, I started taking an adaptogen herb called Ashwagandha. There are many more reasons why this worked for me that I outline in an upcoming chapter. I was desperate to find a solution for the stressed out and anxious life I was living. I needed to calm my anxious overthinking brain, and Ashwagandha helped lessen the stress physically.

The next step was to catch myself doing it and re-center. Sometimes, I physically had to say out loud, "Stop it." Then I would go back to my personal mantras and chant them until my mind calmed down.

The final thing that I have done for years is to journal the repetitive thoughts. When I am struggling or stressed, I journal. It is not anything anyone would ever want to read. It is a mind dump. I literally vomit the words onto the page so they aren't inside me anymore. By writing them down, I can leave them behind. It clears me and re-centers me in a way that nothing else does. As a writer, it also clears the emotions out, so I can move forward with my real writing projects and not be bogged down with the negative thoughts, stresses, and worries that derail all creative thinking. It is the easiest way to reset my anxious brain. I encourage you to try it yourself and see.

The Big Takeaway Question: Do you waste time overthinking or waste effort in overreacting?

Journal on both of these points. If you find yourself in the same boat, develop a plan to pull yourself out of those habits. Reclaim your energy by eliminating these elements in your life.

MICROMANAGING KILLS BRAIN CELLS

Micromanagement is seriously the biggest waste of your time and resources. If you are searching for a truly worthless activity that will leave you stressed, anxious, and worried, this is the one. Thinking your way is always the best is pretty foolish, really, but you can easily trick yourself into thinking that you know the right way to do things. Being someone who was naturally a good planner and who really played the endgame, I thought I always had the right answer, and so my time was consumed in this brain-draining, future-thinking exercise for everyone in my life. Then I manipulated the persons involved to follow my plan because I truly felt it was the path of least pain and in their best interests. The problem is that every person innately wants to make their own choices, and convincing them otherwise becomes a J-O-B.

If you are the master of your domain and you force your opinions onto everyone around you, eventually, there will be a mutiny. An uprising will occur. Tired of following the litany of rules and directions that you set for them, your people will run amuck, making their own decisions, and you know what? That will be okay.

When you micromanage, you are saying to the other person, "I don't trust you enough to make the right decision. I don't believe you are smart enough to consider everything that I have, and I definitely don't believe in your ability to make the right choice." People resent being micromanaged. You do it out of love and concern, but it really says to them that they cannot be trusted. "I am afraid you will make the wrong choice, so I made the choice for you." Teenagers, especially, will fight you on this so very hard. I remember thinking my parents were idiots and that they didn't understand me, and now, I am firmly in the same place with my own kids. I will say that letting them fall has been hard to watch, but the lessons have been so valuable.

The reality is that there are no right choices. When you take away the ability and the option of people to make their own choices, you also take away the lesson life is trying to teach them through it. You stunt their growth because of your own fears. You get in the way of their development.

In order for them to grow into a fully functioning member of society, you need to give them the space to make bad choices, to learn, and to grow from that experience. You need to stay in your own lane and focus on the only one you can control. YOURSELF.

The amazing thing this does for you is that it frees your mental resources from the treadmill of future thinking. You always want to save the ones you love, but you do them no favors by this constant rescue. It's especially hard with your kids because you have been programmed to protect and take care of them. After about thirty-five years of hard-won life experience, you want to save them the grief from all the lessons you were forced to learn, but that teaches them nothing. To grow resilient children into adults, they have to make mistakes, and when you take away all their lessons with micromanagement, and they are eventually faced with real-life lessons, they won't know how to cope.

Micromanaging your own life is even a waste of time. It takes away all the flow and magic of life. You can become so singularly focused that the serendipity doesn't even have a chance to delight you because you have squeezed it out with your fervent micromanagement. Life becomes this constant trudging through the jungle on high alert while scanning for enemies. There is a better way. Let go. Let go of the need to micromanage. Set your intentions. Make your decisions and then let the outcome go. You will still need to show up and take steps toward those goals and intentions, but allow the unknowingness to also have a place in your life. Let the unscripted, naturally flowing, and connecting energy of the universe show you there is more than what you can see or plan. Many times, the natural generosity of the universe shows up bigger for you than your plans ever would. Open yourself up to receiving the awesome things that God has in store for you by not second-guessing everything He wants to give you. Leave space in your life for some improv. It will help calm and heal your brain, and then the decisions you actually have to make will become easier.

And, honestly, it's just not a fun way to live because the script is in constant rewrite. You will spin your wheels endlessly and use all your energy focusing on and worrying about things that never even had any chance of ever happening. Talk about a waste of resources. Fight your habit of micromanaging. Unclench your fists and open your heart and mind to all the possibilities, not just the ones you can see, and watch the magic return to your life.

The Big Takeaway Question: Are you a micromanager? If so, who does this behavior affect?

Journal on the times in your life that you found yourself wrapped up in the mind game of control and micromanaging. Look at the amount of time you have wasted in this mode. How could you repurpose this time better?

THE TWENTY-FOUR-HOUR WALLOW RULE

Bad things happen. For me, they seem to come in waves. Things will be great for a nice long while, then suddenly, the IRS is auditing you, you find out your significant other is unfaithful, you need a breast biopsy, and your dog runs away all in the span of a few weeks. It's easy to get pulled into the downward spiral of a long misery cycle unless you take action to do something about it.

I instituted a twenty-four-hour wallow rule many years ago, and it has been life-changing. When bad news hits, I allow myself to wallow for twenty-four hours, no more. I'll eat the raw cookie dough, take to my bed for *Office* reruns, whine, bitch, and complain. I will take the time to hate that it happened and then do whatever my body tells me to do at the moment to comfort myself. Then, the next day, I work out, take a shower, and move the fuck on.

This gives me a chance to feel the feelings, eat the feelings, proclaim to all of the world that it is not fair, and cry as much as I want about it. It also gives me a deadline for negativity. I have spent my life overcoming punishing negativity. I was raised in a negative, self-limiting household. It was easy to be the victim there, and I hated it. As young as sixteen, I remember searching out the first of the gazillion self-help books I would devour to change my mindset. I learned very early on that mindset is everything. That transforming the space between your ears is the key to getting the life you want. I've been very successful at it, and as a result, when I publicly admitted last year that I struggle with depression, I got many messages, calls, and emails from my circle, who know me as this positive, upbeat, sometimes funny, supremely happy chick. I even was called bright and shiny by a boyfriend.

Life has handed me some difficult cards, and there were several twenty-four-hour wallow breaks in the last several years, but it never diminished my hope that tomorrow will be different. My kids call me the eternal optimist. I think they see my hope as unrealistic and almost cartoon-like with my wide-eyed optimism. It is not because I was born this way. I made myself this way. It is similar to going to the gym and eating well for your body. It's putting the good things in your brain—books, podcasts, and gratitude journaling. It's feeling the sting when things don't go your way, and then getting up to fight the fight the next day and not letting it drag you down. This is a skill you can learn. This is a mindset you can strengthen. The twenty-four-hour wallow rule has helped me get there, time after time.

The twenty-four-hour wallow rule also allows you to feel the feelings and process them, instead of stuffing them and brushing them off. Stuffing your feelings is not the answer. All it does is postpone them and sometimes intensify them. The energy can burn and burn and eventually blow up into something much bigger. By acknowledging them and feeling them right away, the feelings lose their power. You can let it wash over you, feel the feeling, and then move on.

When bad things happen, take the next twenty-four

hours to do whatever you need to do to take care of yourself at the moment. Comfort yourself with whatever makes you feel good or helps you get the feelings out. Go somewhere safe and break things. (Preferably glassware you get from Goodwill, not your mother's china.) Scream into pillows or eat your weight in cookie dough (one day of bad eating won't kill you), then shake it off and move forward. Put a clock on your misery, and then put it away and go out into the world with hope that today will be better because it will.

The Big Takeaway Question: Do you wallow too long?

It is easy to get sucked into negativity, and lots of people live there. By enforcing the twenty-four-hour wallow rule, you won't.

DROP A PLATE

When I was a kid, I went to Adventureland to see the Chinese Acrobats of Teipai and saw an enthralling plate spinning routine that was an insanely accurate model of my early forties. I was enamored, watching them run from plate to plate, spinning the slow ones so fast there were over ten plates spinning at the same time. The exhausted performer feverishly ran from plate to plate, giving it a whirl before running to the next one, in a never-ending energy-draining tornado of effort. It was highly entertaining, but I found out, it's no way to live. Burnout was killing me. I would get up and keep the kid plate spinning, then the work plate, then the side gig plate, then the God plate, then the friends plate, then the husband plate, then the therapy plate, then the dog plate, then the school volunteer plate, then the guilt plate, then the exercise plate. Then repeat. I was taking on too many projects, and it was contributing to this general sense of unrest and fatigue as I ran myself ragged at the expense of keeping everyone else happy.

You have a finite amount of energy on any given day. This may fluctuate depending on how much sleep you got or what your diet is like, but overall, it is a pretty fixed amount. Spinning the plates was tapping me out every day, and something had to change. After my divorce, on a quest to be happier, I decided to take a closer look at all the plates individually, and I dropped one without guilt. This opened up some me-time in my life. This felt good. I started looking for other plates to drop, and I started dropping those, too. I also looked at the plates that were temporary, like driving my kids to endless appointments. Eventually, they would be able to drive themselves. Having an expiration on some of the daily requirements made it easier for me to continue to spin those plates, knowing this plate was temporary. Things would and will change.

I'm an introvert, and some of my plates, especially the ones that included volunteering out of obligation, were draining. I felt guilty for dropping those for the longest time, but out of self-preservation, I allowed myself to try it. This was life-changing because it freed up some of my daily resources that I could repurpose into healing myself. It was more in line with who I naturally am. The church plates pulled on the deepest guilt strings, but I cut myself free anyway. I needed less. Fewer appointments and obligations. I stopped going to parties I didn't want to go to. I didn't apologize or feel inferior anymore about being an introvert. I guarded my time more intensely and started aligning my plates with the life I wanted to live. I accepted my need for quiet time and carved swatches of it out to focus on healing myself and stretching for my goals. The quiet spaces I constructed in my life opened up time for reflection and realigning, and for once, I didn't feel guilty about it.

If you feel run ragged and are having a hard time keeping everything going in your life, taking the time to evaluate plates and dropping some of them is a useful exercise that could save your life. Can your kids take on more responsibility at home? Can they do their laundry? Make their own appointments? Fill out their own paperwork? Teenagers are incredibly savvy and smart when it comes to getting something they want or feel they need. Give them opportunities to step up for themselves while they are living with you. Be a source of information, but let them struggle a bit. Let them figure things out. Don't jump in to save them every second. Let them build their problem-solving skills with you as a safety net in case things go sideways. I was guilty of overdoing for my own fully capable kids out of divorce guilt, but you drastically underestimate what your children can do daily and actually stunt their growth as self-sufficient individuals by overdoing for them.

Can you say no to something or stop going to an activity that you hate? Can you teach someone a skill and then forever delegate it to them instead of doing it for them? Can you trust and have faith that things can be done a different way and all will be okay? The towels do not have to be folded a certain way, and you don't need to reload the dishwasher. Your way is not the only way. Even if it's not okay, it won't change your life significantly if completed differently. In a relationship, are you able to rely on your partner to keep the plate spinning half of the time, or are you the only Chinese Acrobat of Taipei on the payroll? If that is the case, are you willing to accept that? I am not anymore.

Plate spinning is about control and over-extension. It is about doing too much when you crave less. It is about overdoing for fully capable people that actually forces their dependence on you and repeats the cycle of dependence. The only way out is to start dropping plates. Simplify. Stop spreading yourself so micro-thin every day. Be ruthless in the decisions you make about what plates you want to continue to spin. Brutal honesty will set you free instead of wear you out. You may need to redefine what responsibilities are truly yours to continue to carry. You might struggle with a need to be needed. All of these responses point to a deficiency in self-love. With the extra time that you create, you can focus on healing the part of you that is self-destructive. You can forgive yourself for making mistakes, and you can move forward with your second act, purposefully choosing plates that are worth spinning in the first place.

The Big Takeaway Question: What plates are you currently spinning, and which ones can you drop?

Ruthless editing is required to find the resources within to heal yourself and travel your own path to happiness. List your plates and then find ways to drop as many plates as you guiltlessly can.

SLEEPING, EYE TWITCHES, AND PAIN, OH MY!

One of the best gauges of your physical and mental health is taking stock of your physical body. Are you sleeping well? Do you have pain that comes and goes, or maybe just settles in for a nice long time? Your physical body holds the keys to your wellbeing, and that is why you hear things like "follow your gut." Your body knows. Your body is a massive supercomputer, with hard drives full of information imprinted on your DNA. It holds the secrets of your ancestors and relatives. If there is addiction or pain in your family tree, it is written on your DNA, and stress and anxiety become the cornerstones of your cells and mitochondria. Deep generational histories are all there, cataloged and labeled. Your memories can be skewed by your thoughts and perceptions, but you can't lie to your cells. It's science.

During my divorce, I took stock of my physical body and was forced to acknowledge that sleeping had always been an elusive thing for me. I struggled to approach it in a healthy way. I developed an eye twitch that nearly drove me insane and lasted for two years. When it finally disappeared, I almost cried at the miracle. I had accepted it, thinking this is who I am now, but to be free from the insane twitching when life finally settled down was a gift. Just imagine sitting across from me on a first date, watching my eye twitch. It was super hot.

At the end of my marriage, I developed radial myopathy. I was in incredible pain, literal pain with neck and shoulder issues, and sometimes tingling would radiate down my arms. Then, just for fun, it would disappear for a bit to really teach me a lesson, and then mysteriously come raging back, but this time on the other side of my body. Good times. I literally had a pain in the neck, and yet I still didn't put it all together.

When things spiraled out of control with my son, my doctor put me on antidepressants, which made me feel numb and listless, and one of the worst side effects was the incapability of achieving orgasm. Take away a woman's ability for satisfaction and you literally take away her will to live. I had to stop the Lexapro, so I weaned myself off and started a quest to find something better. Something natural.

My sleep patterns were a mess. I eventually would fall asleep after the exhaustion allowed me to, only to wake up four hours later at three in the morning. The stress bunnies immediately popped back up because those fuckers only take a few hours to recharge their batteries. One early morning, I Googled something to the effect of, why am I waking up at 3 am every night? This Google quest led me to an article that stated if you were waking up at 3 or 4 am every morning on your own, you were steeped in anger and sadness. I longed to sleep in, to be able to unplug and shut off the internal dialogue, stress, and worry. I desired to let go, but my body would not let me.

On a quest to take better care of myself and to survive when my life clearly wasn't working, I researched and studied. I got massages and diffused essential oils. I ordered whole-food vitamins. In my search to find a natural cure for anxiety, I came across an herb called Ashwagandha. It promised to help with so many of my current ailments that I thought it was worth a seventeen-dollar investment. During my messy divorce, there was a constant sensation of never being able to take a full breath. There was a tightness in my chest, and all my nerves were stretched like a drum. I was so tightly wound that nearly everything would set me off.

One more desperate early morning a few days later, after reading all the articles I could find, I added Ashwagandha to my amazon cart. Two days later, it arrived. I started taking the Ashwagandha before bed, and in a week, I went from sleeping four hours to sleeping six and then eight. For an insomniac like me, it was nothing short of a miracle. I noticed the tightness in my chest begin to loosen. I seemed better able to cope, even when things got heated and stressful. I gave a half-dose to my sweet anxious daughter. It made things easier for her, and there were more jokes and smiles coming from her. It truly changed our lives for the better.

It is an adaptogen herb, something that helped calm down the supercharged life I was living. Stress will destroy your system, but taking an adaptogen herb can help build it back up. I am not a doctor, so if you choose to take this, please clear it with your doctor. It is not the answer for everyone, and can even work against you. Do the research, ask your doctor, and make the decision for yourself. All I know is that, when I started taking it, life became more manageable. Maybe because I was sleeping better, I had more energy and resources to better handle the problems that were coming my way. Maybe I was able to take those deeper breaths, so it eased the ton of bricks that had been laid on my chest. I didn't fucking care. All I knew was that I felt better. That was the only barometer for me. Did it work?

Emotional pain manifests physically. If you are in pain, look to resolve the emotional pain in your life. Look to heal your soul, your mind, and your body, instead of just focusing always on the physical. When you get to the root of it, healing the emotions will heal the body and put you into a state of goodness. If you have pain that keeps returning, look inward. If you are in a relationship and you find yourself physically feeling tightness and pain in your chest, neck, or head, your body is telling you it is not the right one. If you develop an eye twitch, or neck and back issues, your emotional pain is screaming for healing.

Listen to your own body. If you meditate, take a few breaths and reconnect to your center. Your body is highly intelligent, a supercomputer inside a soft, fleshy shell. Take stock of the hints your body is sending to you. Don't ignore the signals it is sending. Do your own research and find ways to heal yourself. Yoga, breathing, long walks in nature, all the things that people have known for centuries work. Build your own toolbox of restoration.

The Big Takeaway Question: What is your body trying to tell you?

Take a physical inventory. Do you feel chronic pain? Where? How are you sleeping? Is there tension in your body? Do you feel tightness? Do you feel constricted? Look to heal the underlying emotions of your physical pain. The right relationship is restorative. It brings you peace, not problems. Your body is sending you messages. Tune in and listen.

ALIGNMENT AND ADJUSTMENTS

Why is it easier to go to the chiropractor than to see a therapist? Both heal our bodies and get us back in alignment, yet it is so much more socially acceptable to seek out healing for physical pain. Like it or not, there is still a stigma that prevents many people from seeking out a solution for mental pain.

When you are in alignment, everything works better. You move better, you think better, and you sleep better. Six years ago, I started getting intermittent numbness and tingling down my arms as a stress reaction to the painful events in my life. I got to the point where I had to walk around with my hand raised for most of the day on bad days because it was the only way to make the nerve happy.

I needed to get the nerves to settle down, so I sought out chiropractic adjustments. They would help, and then I would stop going and get back out of alignment, and the cycle would repeat. As my life would get more stressful, and the cortisol would hit all-time new highs, the symptoms would return and the adjustments would begin again.

When you are living with physical pain, most people only

treat the physical pain. I have learned there is almost always an underlying emotional component to it. Physical pain is a sign that there are deeper things going on that need to be adjusted. The pain was a marker for the terrible, soul-sucking relationships I had attracted into my life. It was a stress reaction to never feeling safe in any relationship with a man. It was my body screaming at me to listen, that something was gravely wrong. Something needed to change right now, and the pain was the warning bell.

The biggest correlation I couldn't grasp until recently is that your emotions also need alignment. Your soul needs adjustments and alignments as much as, or more than, your spine. Putting a Band-Aid on your body is a temporary solution, but what you really need is to address the underlying stress and painful emotional patterns you are engaging in that often manifest in physical ways. You have to be willing to dig deep because some of these issues go incredibly deep. You have to unearth generational emotional pain, stressors, and addictions.

I started working with an energy healer for the last several months, and this experience has changed me. It has shown me that the experiences of our family of origin profoundly affect what is currently going on in our lives. For so long, I had so much guilt and so much pain around my son's mental health and addiction issues. After learning it was inevitable, there was a certain kind of freedom and peace because, for so long, I felt strained, sad, and guilty for not doing enough, for not being there enough or demanding enough from him. The truth is that he was destined to be born this way. His father is an addict, his grandfather was an addict, and so it is part of his generational DNA. It didn't matter where we lived, what music he listened to, or if we got a divorce. The end result would have been the same. Is it something he can overcome? Yes, but that will require him to do the work to free himself. The anger and addiction in him are so deeply entrenched in centuries of familial DNA. It needs to be released, but this is work and alignment he will need to take on himself.

When you get away from emotional alignment, things feel off. They feel bad, and they feel forced. You need to get back to the truth of who you are and use your emotions to understand what they are telling you. Emotions are good. They can almost be interpreted like tea leaves because they leave clues about what is or is not working in your life. If you are stuck in fear, anger, jealousy, or shame, these are signs that you are out of alignment with who you are and what you want. If you are in the flow and feel good, if you feel happy, clear, or joyful, this is a sign that you are on the right track, and so you can continue to use your emotions to gauge whether it is time for an adjustment.

Every decision you make that pulls you away from your true self pulls you out of alignment. Some of these decisions will be small, and proportionally, the pain will be small. Some of them will be huge, and the suffering will be huge. Instead of letting the emotion wreak havoc in your life, a better thing to ask is what is this feeling trying to teach me? Where am I out of alignment? Discovering this will help you make different decisions that align with what you want and will get you closer to the happiness you want to feel.

It is time that you look at the pursuit of healing your mental health as a task that is as necessary as healing your physical health. It might even be more important. Staying in alignment mentally requires a lifetime of check-ins and attention, but it is some of the most important work you will ever undertake.

I have been in therapy for years, but I didn't start going until I was over forty and the house was on fire. I pushed the work I needed to do away, to deal with later, until I couldn't anymore. Don't be like me. Do yourself a favor and embark on your own quest to heal yourself through therapy, journaling, or long walks in nature. Kick away the shame and embrace your desire to become healthier, to do the work of keeping your body and your soul in alignment. If you put it off or ignore the call, it will wait for you. Someday, the consequences you leave unchecked will come for you, if necessary so painfully that it will burn your entire life to the ground to get your attention. Do yourself a favor and start before your life is a total loss. Start now on your journey of self-healing and improvement.

The Big Takeaway Question: Where are you out of alignment?

Alignment comes in many forms. Take a loving look at your weak spots and find out what they are trying to tell you.

PROCRAPINATION: THE SUBTLE ART OF NEVER REACHING YOUR DREAMS

Yep, you read that right. Procrapination. It really is crappy. It is a form of self-sabotage that is easy to engage in because there are so many ways to do it. I love to write, but I find that if I don't get at it first thing in the morning, then I can come up with a million excuses and ways to delay it. *I'll start after this episode of Breaking Bad. I need to wash my sheets. The dog needs a walk. I need to clean my desk so my mind is less cluttered.* There are a million things I can invent as excuses to put off the most important things I need to do.

What is at the heart of procrapination is fear. Fear is everywhere! It's a literal fear buffet out there. When you put off something important, something that you need to do, you are letting fear win. You are saying, "I am not getting the mammogram because my mom died from breast cancer, and I am afraid of what the results will be." When I don't write and get off track with my goals to publish my book, I am saying, "I am afraid to finish because, if I finish, then I need to put it out there, and then what happens if it is a gigantic failure?

It seems like the bigger the goal, the harder it is to stop procrapinating. It takes discipline to push through when the doubts cue up, or you'd rather go to a party instead of finish writing a chapter. Fear is that loud liar in your brain screaming for attention. When the fear is holding you down, take a smaller approach. Tell yourself you are just going to do this one thing. That may or may not be a lie, because you might find yourself in the zone after doing the one thing and find you can keep going for hours.

Doing one thing in the morning, for me, is the secret to success. There is less resistance in the morning because that loud liar in my brain likes to sleep in. Once I tackle that one thing, I find that the rest of my day flows so much better. I get to build on the tiny bit of success I created for myself. It sets the whole day up for victory. This is why I exercise in the morning. If I don't, then the chances are really good that it won't happen, that something earth-shattering will take greater precedence, like having to take a Facebook quiz to see if my personality type is compatible with the guy I am dating. Or finding the perfect potato salad recipe on Pinterest. The rabbit holes of my life are many, and I can endlessly find ways to kill a day that don't get me any closer to who I want to be.

Procrapination is easy to identify. It is anytime something gets in between you and your goals. It comes in little and big ways. Like all bad habits, when compounded daily, weekly, and yearly, it can lead to a life so off course and out of alignment with who you say you want to be that intense dissatisfaction will be the only result. The way out of this is to take action. Do something that you are putting off. At first, it will feel forced, like the kiss your mom forced you to give your Great Aunt Ruth with the chin whiskers when you were fourteen. As you work on projects that you have been putting off, there will be a shift in momentum. You will start to gain energy from showing up and putting in effort toward your life's work. You will feel more confident and more capable, and not as inclined to binge-watch Netflix while eating brownie batter.

Another more insidious form of procrastination comes in the form of perfectionism. You can endlessly toil to make it better, telling yourself and others that it isn't ready yet. I am a big believer in creating a minimum viable product. Do your thing as well as you can in an allotted time space and then put it out there. It will never be perfect. Nothing ever is. The pursuit of perfectionism will detour your success, yet give you the ability to take the high road. Ditch perfectionism and get comfortable with the eighty percent. If it's eighty percent there, you're usually good, unless you're a pilot or a brain surgeon.

It's easy to stay in a rut of nothingness, of getting home and putting on the stretchy pants and procrapinating. Forcing yourself through the early awkward stages will build muscles you can use to keep going when you don't really feel like it or when you tell yourself, "I've been doing so good, I deserve a break." When you take hard steps toward your goals and dreams, it will be exciting and energizing. It will feel like a great workout. At the end of it, you are happy you did it and you feel stronger, but it was work. Hard work.

The Big Takeaway Question: What are you putting off? Why?

It's not enough to have a dream. You also have to show up and work for it. You have to put in the time and do the hard things. Outline the next few baby steps you need to take. Build your own momentum toward what you really want. Stop the procrapination.

YOU CAN'T MAKE EVERYONE HAPPY

Many young women grew up like I did, in the people-pleasing time of the eighties, when we were groomed to be a good girl. Where we were taught to be agreeable and self-sacrificing and generous. It doesn't take much to condition a little child to do as she is told and how she is told to do it. I was a girl like that, driven to please my parents, to do the things that would make them happy, never considering what I really wanted to do. My relationships were exercises that deeply ingrained this behavior even more. "I don't know. What do you want to do?" became an automatic answer.

My marriage was the same. Trying to take care of everyone else's needs was an exercise in futility as I tried and tried, wearing myself out to cover the bases of everyone else. The husband, the kids, my clients, and then getting up to do it again the next day.

The failure of many things, including my marriage, taught me that I was killing myself to make everyone else happy. When it all came to a screeching halt, I discovered the real truth was that the only person I needed to make happy was myself. Most of the time, making other people happy required me to sacrifice. Oftentimes, I was willing to sacrifice nearly everything in my quest for outward acceptance and happiness. The hardest lesson to learn was that other people's happiness was fickle and fleeting, and then I was forced back in performance mode like a circus clown trying to make them happy again. About this time, I just said, "Fuck it. I give up." That was honestly the thing that saved me.

People pleasers are usually some of the most miserable people you will ever meet because they put their happiness in someone else's hands. That never works out well for anyone. It becomes a vicious cycle of effort and failure that is exhausting. Instead of pleasing other people, go please yourself. All that effort and energy you put into pleasing the people in your life should be redirected to making yourself happy. Take yourself out for ice cream. Spend an hour in the bead section at the fabric store because the strings of beautiful beads look like candy. Walk in nature or, better yet, on the beach if you're near one. Even in the middle of winter, I have had magical experiences that have restored me that cost absolutely nothing, just the time to do them. Invest in your own happiness one little lovely experience at a time.

For me, when I need to replenish, the fastest way I can do that is to make something. A cake, a garden, a photograph, a journal entry. Creating things—anything—is a way of filling myself back up and getting back in touch with that childlike happiness. Two-year-olds are naturally happy and some of the most selfish creatures ever created. They color, they dance when they hear music, and they ask for what they want. They pitch a fit when their needs aren't being met, and they do not even begin to know how to people please. They snort and laugh and, when they are good and pissed, flop on the ground face down screaming. Two-year-olds don't try to make anyone happy. They are just in it for their own amusement. If you are a chronic people-pleaser, you must channel your inner two-year-old. The model of self-happiness and selfishness is something you may need to relearn. At first, it will feel strange, but I'd like to encourage you to push past it and try it for a while.

You are in charge of you. Sure, people and circumstances can come into your life and make you situationally happy for a time, but the real baseline of your happiness is self-driven. You can cultivate happiness in your heart by finding the good in every day. Even the soul-sucking ones always have a glimmer of good if you look for it. Happiness is a choice. It is you choosing to see the good in every situation. It is you choosing to give people the benefit of the doubt when they have wronged you. It is you making a conscious decision to let the little things go and focus on what is working in your life.

Take responsibility for your own happiness. Don't put it into the hands of the guy you are dating, or your children, or your friends. That is a recipe for resentment and frustration. Don't be a happiness procrastinator. Don't tell yourself, "I will be happy when…" and make it conditional according to the job you have or the person you date. Those things are likely to disappear, plunging you into a state of despair. Instead, cultivate happiness in a wider sense that doesn't depend on any outside circumstance to be present.

If you find yourself in a place of sadness and sorrow, take on the job of making yourself happy. Listen to the internal tug on your heartstrings and follow where it leads. If you don't know where to start, get quiet and wait. Eventually, a little bit of curiosity will bubble up. Follow those bubbles in whatever direction calls to you.

Without joy, wonder, and curiosity, life becomes a bleak exercise, marching endlessly toward death. I know that sounds harsh, but it is coming for all of us. Wouldn't it be much better to have oodles of happy memories to entertain you when you're in the nursing home? Don't let your life go on autopilot. Live with intention. Line up as much as you can with what makes you happy and what sparks joy in your heart. Life is better when you're happy. Make your happiness a priority.

The Big Takeaway Question: Are you in charge of your happiness? What ways can you add more happiness into your life?

Journal little ways to find happiness in your life and chase them wherever they lead.

CREATION BUILDS WORLDS OR DESTROYS THEM

Want the secret to happiness? Go create something. Anything, even if it's bad. Happiness is in the process, not the finished product. I believe that we are creators, created by the Ultimate Creator. It is our natural nature. Children are the best at this already. They play, they create stories in their heads, they color outside the lines without a care in the world, they wrap a blanket around their shoulders and transform themselves into superheroes. Then we and society beat them down with our words and our actions until the creativity and playfulness are gone in favor of creating worker bees who are effective but not happy.

I love to make things. When I was a kid, I bought myself oil paints with my allowance and would lock myself in my bedroom for hours, getting slightly high on turpentine and linseed oil, and turn out some truly terrible paintings. My greatest desire was to move to Paris and become a famous artist. Bob Ross was my hero, and in some ways he still is, but now I appreciate his gentle approach to life, his generous spirit, and his fabulous afro. I mean, not many white men can pull that off.

When I was walking through the campground we stayed at as kids, I would pick up acorns and make little people out of them, then I attempted wood burning and carving, and I wrote stories with cheesy romantic leads. I was never a master at any of them, but it didn't matter. I was in the zone. I was creating.

One of my very favorite things to do when I was in middle school was a field trip to the Waterloo Center of the Arts. At least once a year we got to go on a tour of an exhibit, and then we got to spend a few hours learning a new art form that went hand in hand with the exhibit. One year, we learned rosemaling, a Norwegian swirly style of painting that was something I was terrible at, but it still was an incredibly enjoyable way to waste an afternoon.

As an adult, a day of day drinking and crafting can perk my spirits up like nothing else can. Just me and the glue gun, one with life, burning my fingers but loving every minute. If you are stuck, and it happens to all of us, the easiest way to get unstuck is to create. Creation comes in so many forms. It might be restoring that '67 Mustang in the garage, or setting up your home automation to greet you when you walk in the house as Lord Sugarsnatch of the Iowa Realm. It's painting the bedroom or hand-lettering art for over the bed. It is scrapbooking your millions of photos into books you pour over again and again if you're sentimental like me.

There is no right way to create, and there is no judgment. It is getting into the groove of life and losing yourself for hours in something that makes you feel alive and free. What makes you feel this way might make someone else yawn, and that is okay. It is about *you*. What can you do to play, to change your space or place for the better, to make your world prettier or easier or more fun? What can you transform? Whether it is painting, or tiling your backsplash, or repurposing a dresser as a pet bed, or getting your hands dirty in the garden with flowers or veggies. You owe it to yourself to get out there and do it. You owe it to yourself to set aside some time every week, and eventually, every day, to play.

You may say, "But Ninya, I don't have time for that." That is a lie. You do. Everyone does. It is a matter of making this time important enough to you that you will do what it takes to keep this obligation for yourself. If you are stuck, try this. Set aside one hour during the week and create something. Anything. Whatever you want. Keep this appointment like you would a prepaid massage appointment, not like a root canal appointment that you will wiggle out of if you wake up with a hangnail. You will see that not only will it make you happier, but you will find yourself working through the problems that need solutions in your mind as your fingers are occupied gluing on sequins, or making the perfect tree line. Your subconscious computer-like left brain will continue to crank through solutions, even while your right brain is enjoying the ride and creating the perfect guitar riff. It really is healthy and good to occupy both sides of your brain at the same time. The best breakthroughs seem to come from this calmer creative state. Even if your life is in turmoil, you will be more equipped to weather the storm with this break for your brain.

Creation can also be negative. You can create scenarios in your brain that fuel your anxiety and negativity. You can create stories in your mind about your boyfriend cheating when he was just pre-occupied with a work issue and forgot to kiss you when he left for work. Keeping your creation in positive pursuits helps keep it too busy to concoct crazy. You are a creative being, and you are driven to create. One way or another, this compulsion will manifest amazing new things like craft projects, scrapbooks, and photographs, or you will create stress, drama, and pain. An idle mind is a scary thing and all that is necessary to get the anxiety merry go round cued up for another terrifying ride. Keep your mind occupied in healthy, creative ways. Try anything that speaks to you. Try new things. You never know when you chase a creative rabbit down a rabbit hole where it will lead.

I struggle with depression. I have since I was sixteen. It comes and goes with the stresses of life. Now that I am older, I can see the correlation between depression and creativity. There are always two scenarios. I can get out of bed, go thrifting, and bring home something I can transform with spray paint, or I can stay in bed and write stories in my head that I am doomed and the people in my life don't love me. I used to be very prolific at paranoia cinema—a theatrical experience completely in my head, featuring heroes and villains pulled from my own life, engaged in dramatic plot twist after plot twist. It was nearly a 3D experience, so vivid, so lifelike that these scenarios sometimes jumped from my mind into reality. Talk about using my creative powers for evil! Don't do that. Use your powers for good. One way or another, your brain will create something. You get to decide if you want it to create heaven or a very personalized version of hell.

They call it a creative outlet for a reason. There is energy that needs expression, that needs to flow through you. Some of the angriest and most hateful people are the ones who have creative dreams that have gone unrealized. When creativity is stagnant or blocked, it creates tension, fear, resentment, and anger. It reduces life to soul-sucking obligatory tasks, leaving no time for chasing dreams that make the soul come alive and play. Creativity is playful, whimsical, and childlike. When we ignore it, it becomes an insubordinate and naughty child that needs to be punished.

You have responsibilities. I get that. We all do. There is always space to fit creativity into the nooks and crannies of your life. The more nooks you find, the happier you will be. Even in a life chock full of responsibilities, you can find time to carve out one hour a week. Most people who do this find themselves sneaking away and finding more ways to commune with their creativity after they have a taste. Like an illicit lover who they sneak away to savor and touch, it becomes a craving so intense you cannot ignore it. But unlike a torrid affair, this will not destroy your life. Instead, it will breathe life back into it.

Creation can build your world or destroy it, and every day the choice is yours, so which is it?

The Big Takeaway Question: What are your favorite healthy creative outlets? What are your favorite forms of play?

Journal on this question and, if you want extra credit, write about some times in your life when your creativity went into destruction mode. What led you there? Is there something you are curious about, that you want to learn and discover about yourself? Have you thought, "That sounds intriguing! or "I would love to try that!" Write down those hints and be open to the experiences that start being drawn into your life.

THE DREAM

I have always been a head in the clouds, shoot for the moon kind of girl. Since nearly birth, I have devoured self-help books by the basketful. At a particularly low period, I would go to Barnes and Noble and sit in a comfortable chair and read entire books that I couldn't afford to buy, desperate to free myself from my parents' negative thinking. Every year when January rolls around, I am nearly giddy with excitement, dreaming about my new goals and writing them down, in list form so I can go back to them daily and remind myself why I am fighting the good fight.

I dream about the house I want to build, the trips I want to take, the healthy meals and incredible skincare regimen I will be able to partake in when things change financially and money is flowing again into my life. Even at my lowest lows, when I had to take a lunch lady job to fill the need for health insurance, I never stopped dreaming and visualizing what I wanted in my attempt to attract it into my life. It's especially important for people who are at a low to dream. When things look bleak, that's when you need it most because a dream is really just hope itemized. It is a belief that things won't stay ugly forever, but that you can and will correct your situation soon if you just focus on where you are headed.

You have to dream big, and don't let anyone tell you otherwise. Don't look around at your current circumstances and rewrite your dreams in order to be realistic. Fuck realistic. Realistic blows goats. It minimizes your worth and tells you to play smaller. It gives you a sliver of the pie when you want the whole fucking thing. Don't settle for a taste. Dream about eating so much you have to lie on the couch with a belly ache.

I am writing this during a time when things are transitional. When the dream of building a house disappeared in the nuclear bomb of Covid-19. Initially, I was crushed. It was hard to swallow that my dream of building a house would be on hold because I wanted it so bad. I still do. The timing wasn't quite right, and as a result, some major things shifted, and the city we wanted to build in isn't even where we want to live now. That was a blessing in disguise. The unfulfillment of that dream will actually work out better in the end. I still dream, now more than ever, that my books will allow me to create a beautiful life for me and my kids. I dream about what it will feel like, finally getting the opportunity to walk through the door of the house that my books built. I dream about having the freedom of time, to be able to let go of my lunch lady gig, secure in the knowledge that my writing fully supports the incredible life I dream about living.

I dream about Japan and Greece and Chile and all the incredible places I yearn to discover with my kids and my love. I dream about the endless adventures my hard work will provide. I dream about being able to help my children secure their futures in whatever healthy way makes them whole and happy. I dream about helping them create their own roots and giving them the support to chase their own creative endeavors. I dream about security and peace, things that have been so elusive, but that will be borne now out of my writing. I dream about getting a call from Oprah Winfrey herself, and the screaming that will follow when one of my books is selected for her book club.

Your dream is personal. It is something you should carefully curate, leaving room for things to morph and change as you morph and change. It should inspire you to jump out of bed in the morning, give you the gas to keep going when you're running on fumes but at the end of an important deadline. Your dream is your roadmap of the kind of experience you want to have on earth and who you want to have it with. It is playing with the idea of what if everything went right? What would that look like?

Dream the big dream, fearlessly and without your inner critic telling you it will never happen. Write your dream down, then your ideal day, and review them daily. Seeing this information every day helps your brain to see connections consciously and subconsciously. It scans your reality constantly for people and opportunities that could help you make them come true. Get clear on every little detail of your dream and understand why you want it in the first place, how it will impact your life for the better. Visualize yourself making it come true. Close your eyes first thing in the morning, create a movie in your head where your biggest dream comes true, and let this thought flood you with happiness and excitement. This is a beautiful way to intentionally start your day.

Dream every day. Dream when you are stuck in the pit of despair and things seem bleak because that is when you need it most. Share your dream sparingly, and only with deeply trusted friends and family. Do not let their anxieties of not achieving their own dreams spill out onto you. Do not buy into their fear of their own dreams not coming true, so this must mean neither will yours. Hold your dream in the deepest parts of your heart, protected from these types of people. Work quietly toward it, building courage as you go to take bigger steps toward your dream. This is how you work to make your dream come true. At the same time, leave space for the magic, for the unknown component to pop in and blow your mind. For Oprah Winfrey to call and touch her golden finger to your project.

Be a dreamer filled with hope that things are shifting and that life is getting ready to blow your mind. Because, when you start thinking like this, it will.

The Big Takeaway Question: What is your dream?

Journal the hell out of this. Be specific. Attach numbers and measurements to the things you seek. Write it all down and then take thirty more minutes to write out your ideal day. Where do you live? What do you do? What do you eat? Who do you do it with? Nail that dream down to concrete things. Your brain will crunch away at solutions to deliver what you want. Everything starts with a dream. Dream BIG!

YOU'RE NEVER GOING TO BE DONE

You're never going to be done until you die. Then you are done. Until then, life is an endless series of lessons and joy and suffering, and you get to control how much fun you have along the way. I used to have this endless to-do list in my head that had to be accomplished before I could let myself be happy. First, I had to have the right job and then I would be happy. Then it was finding the right apartment and then I would be happy, and then I had to find the right guy and then I would be happy. But the nature of humans, as soon as we accomplish something or get the thing, we only enjoy it a split second before we are onto the next thing we need before we let ourselves be happy.

This is an exhausting way to live that sucks the joy out of life. Your work is never done, and so you have to find the time or make the time to have fun along the way or you will just burn out and get nothing accomplished. How do you do that? You look for things that make you feel good. This is different for everyone, and it doesn't have to be extravagant or even cost anything at all. It is taking the time in a moment to do something that makes you smile or makes someone else smile.

It is the constant striving toward goals that can lead to burnout, and then striving toward the next goal when, in reality, you need to savor every step of the way. Lately, I have been trying to savor little moments. Like when I crawl into bed and smell the fresh clean sheets, or being grateful for the soft pillow I get to sink into and relax. It is watching all the doggies frolicking at the dog park behind my apartment. It's letting the dark chocolate slowly melt on my tongue and watching comedy specials with my daughter where we both laugh at the same terrible things. These are the moments that matter.

I used to get up and write myself a ridiculously long to-do list. My list was so impossibly ambitious and time-consuming, no man could ever strive to complete it in a twenty-four-hour period. As a result, I was constantly stressed, worried, and living in a never enough state. I finally got off my own back and started making my to-do list on a 3x5 index card. It's like forcing yourself to eat your dinner on a saucer to lose weight. The smaller the paper, the smaller the list. So, at the start of every day, I list 3-5 things that must be done, and when I am done with those, I can consider it a productive day. Let's eat caramels to celebrate.

As a Type A person, it is hard to just relax and be. Part of learning to be in the flow is to work toward what you want, as long as it is healthy, but the other half that is harder for Type A's is to release and relax. Let it come to you. Let it find you. It's easy for someone like me to work and work and work, burning themselves out. I have always said that, out of all the -aholics, being a workaholic is the best one. As I have gotten older, I see and feel the difference between keeping up a frenzied pace, laser-focused on what I want to happen, and allowing it to happen. I have had to remind myself that the true magic exists in unclenching my fist a little and letting it come to me. I used to be so tightly wound and controlled that I killed my share of sweet little rabbity ideas. Just call me Lennie.

Now, I realize that there is a balance between the work I need to do, and the relaxing and allowing that need to happen. While you are relaxing, the only thing you are required to do is anything that feels good. You can take a short nap or a long one. You can make cookie dough and eat it for breakfast. You can buy yourself a little air plant to hang in the window in your bedroom. There really is no end to the little things you can do to make yourself happy in the quiet moments of releasing and allowing. There may be an adjustment for you. You may feel a smidge guilty. This means you need to do it *more.*

You're never going to be done. You are on an endless journey with yourself. Yes, other people will come into your life. Some will stay, and some will hurt you so much you never think you'll survive it. Yet, at any moment in time, you can choose and make a decision to do something that makes you feel good. In those moments, you can relax into allowing the universe to do its part while you enjoy the sun on your face. Work then release. Work then release. This is the biggest key to a healthier balanced life and one I wish I could have figured out years ago. You're never going to be done, so learn to enjoy life every step of the way.

The Big Takeaway Question: What ways can you interject fun into your life?

Find little things to make yourself feel good, whether it is sitting in the sun, taking your dog for a walk, painting your toenails, or planning a trip. Make a list of these good feeling things and then pepper them into your life.

DON'T CHEAT

Don't cheat yourself or rush the process in your hurry or desire to find someone to share your life with. You cannot properly heal yourself inside of a new relationship, and it is selfish to ask the new person to wade through your emotional discovery and healing process. Not to mention, like attracts like. Unhealthy people attract unhealthy mates. Only when you take the time to fix yourself and properly heal will you be able to recognize a healthy partner.

That advice sucks. I totally get it. I didn't take it, but sister, I wish I had. I ran right out after my divorce and distracted myself with back to back relationships, and pain and destruction followed. Not to mention, my kids were now along for the ride. They witnessed every misstep, every low point, all the tears and anguish and anxiety I was in, and it hurt them deeply.

The steps take time. Uncovering your true self is not a quick process that is linear. It is a windy road down dark ravines you do not want to go down. Taking an inventory of where you are and realigning with what you want and what you need takes a level of patience and mindfulness that takes time to develop. I wish I could tell you there was a way to fast track it, but there isn't. It is you, taking the time to dig deep and uncover the truth of who you are and then becoming confident enough in yourself to know you can't go back. To draw a line in the sand and say to yourself, "Enough. No more settling. No more accepting less than what I deserve."

When you skip steps, you will find yourself allowing bad behavior or letting it slide, and if you have ever raised a two-year-old, you know what a monster you can create in that kind of environment. You deserve the time to carefully consider your life, to look at the past you have lived through, not with shame or regret but in acknowledgment of the lessons that you have learned. You can't skip to the good stuff. If it was easy, everyone would be doing it already, and no one would need this book.

Only when you can see yourself for the treasure you are will you be able to draw the person into your life that can appreciate your beauty. Someone who will be able to appreciate all your facets, every quirk and personality trait that makes you so gorgeous. You are a treasure, and chances are, everyone else in your life sees it already. Now, you just need to convince yourself.

A woman who is in love with life glows. She is magnetic and powerful in an animalistic way. The smile on her face reaches every molecule of her being. She is beauty. She is light. She is impossible to ignore.

Don't compare your healing process to anyone else's. It's gonna take as long as it needs to take. You'll know when you're ready because of the ease of the decision. It will not be based on need. You will be in a place to take care of yourself completely. You will be financially, physically, and mentally secure. You won't need to couple up for any other reason except that you want to share your overflow with someone.

You want a partner to enhance what is already working. Thinking finding a partner will fix anything is a bad place to begin something that you want to last. It is not your relationship's job to fix anything or fill anything that is lacking. It is your job to fix and fill. When you approach your next relationship from this place of fulfillment, it is so much easier to attract the right person because you will be drawn to each other in health instead of need. This is the place where love thrives.

The Big Takeaway Question: Are you truly ready?

Only you will know when you are ready to add a partner to your life. If you aren't quite there, don't shame or blame yourself. Simply continue to work on what is lacking, where you feel vulnerable or needy. Then continue to dig and find the source of this pain and heal it. Forgive and let go. Learn and develop.

If you are ready, then this is an exciting time. You know who you are. You have seen your missteps and have forgiven yourself for making them. You have standards, good ones that encourage good behavior and that are in line with who you are. You are ready and I, for one, am so proud of you because I know firsthand how much work it takes to heal yourself.

THEN HIM

SAFETY FIRST AND GETTING BACK IN THE DATING POOL

Truly, if you are putting yourself out there, there are a few things you need to think about right off the bat. The internet is a dangerous place where people can hide and lie. Take precautions like checking out a person's public life through social media before you meet. I always asked for the full name and birthdate of a guy before I would consent to meet a stranger on a date. Then I would go to Iowa Courts Online and look him up. This did two things. One, it immediately eliminated the bad guys. And two, if they refused, they either had something to hide or they weren't interested enough. In today's day and age, you can't be too careful. It is public record, after all, and it saves you from attracting a predator with a dangerous past. They do exist, so you need to be careful.

Always meet someone you don't know in a public place. Don't let them be chivalrous and pick you up because this could be a way to find out where you live. They can pick you up on date two or three. Meet them on your own turf and drive yourself. It also makes sure you don't get tipsy enough to do anything stupid that you will regret later. (See, girl? I got you.) Also, always let someone know where you are going and who you are meeting. It's just a precaution.

Lastly, listen to your intuition. If there is any fear of any kind, either when you text or in person, listen to it. Your mind is incredibly capable of ensuring your survival. If you have an inkling, a tiny feeling, or a whisper of something not being quite right, it usually is accurate.

If a prospective person that you're messaging passes all these tests, then get together for a face-to-face, in-person meeting as soon as possible. The only accurate way to judge chemistry is to physically share space with the person you are dating. Do not endlessly text them for weeks, months, or years. If they are messaging you but never want to meet in real life, run away. Don't waste any of your precious time engaging in this pseudo-relationship. Cat-fishing happens, but you can avoid the shame and embarrassment if you press to meet in person and they refuse or come up with endless excuses. I encourage you to be flirty and bold and say something like, "Are we going to meet up in person, or are you just going to text me forever?" Then suggest a place to do just that.

If the man is too busy to meet, he is not your guy. If a guy is interested, he will make the time if you are important to him. Even the most successful, C Level career man will move mountains to be with you. If he can't make time in the early stages when men are tripping over themselves and going out of their way to woo you, then do you think, when you are six months in, he will change? The answer is no. Cut him loose and move on to the next one until you find the guy who will make you a priority. It is unnatural for a man attracted to a woman to stay away from her physically. If he is not making an effort to see you in person, he is not your guy.

The right thing is easy. It is easy in every aspect of your life. Whether we are talking about buying a house or finding the right guy, the right path flows and is simple. It works without the massive drain of effort. Too much of the time, when you are forcing that square peg into your round hole, you are so sure and so focused on making it fit that you don't see the fundamental problem. It will never fit unless you grind it down and change it to fit your round hole. And when you are done, you will still have something you forced into submission, not something that slips easily and effortlessly into place but something that kinda works but still gets stuck from time to time.

The massive amount of energy that you drain in the forcing process is a waste of your resources. Think about how much brainpower you would instantly free up if you accepted that simple truth. The right thing is easy, so if this is too hard, it's not the right thing.

Relationships take effort. I am not saying it's all sunshine and rainbows all the time in the right relationship. I am saying that, overwhelmingly, the ease should be present at least 80% of the time. You should be allies working together like a well-oiled team on the Amazing Race, not nitpicking and undermining each other at the drop of a hat. Arguing over the little battles wastes all your energy for when the big ones that are worth fighting come. And they will come for every couple. If you waste all your energy waging the small battles, you'll lose the war.

Be safe, be open, and be healthy. Then you will attract quality human beings into your life.

The Big Takeaway Question: What's his full name and birthdate?

I am not kidding. Check him out before you meet. Tell your friends who you are seeing and where you are going. Safety first.

RELATIONSHIP ADDICTION

Falling in love is addictive. It literally changes your brain chemistry and makes you do crazy things because you're so googly-eyed. I have been there, sister. That rush of excitement that drives you wild. The constant texting back and forth and honeymoon phase that makes you feel wanted and loved. Each text is a little dopamine hit, complete with butterflies, that keeps you coming back for more, ignoring sleep because it is so heady and all-consuming. The will he or won't he, not knowing, bliss-filled passion of getting to know someone new is exciting. Captivating. Holds you spellbound. I was under that spell for a nice long time. I know how awesome it feels to have that rush of desire, the quaking loins and heaving bosoms. (I might have slipped into my mom's Harlequin romances there for a second. Sorry.)

For me, it became a sort of drug that I craved, and because I didn't love myself yet, this drug took the edge off and distracted me from what I was really supposed to be working on. Then reality would set in when the person I was dating started to show their true colors and make those red flags apparent. The dopamine would slow down, settling into the natural state of the relationship, and I would be off to chase the next hit.

Addictions are bad for you and come in all sorts of shapes and sizes you can use to distract yourself. That first hit of dopamine coursing through your veins is what keeps the junkies coming back for more. It's hot and sexy and all-consuming, and that is precisely why it can become an addiction.

The issue becomes a problem when you go from one high to the next, chasing that forever fleeting feeling without detoxing between substances and giving yourself a chance to sober up. I was extremely guilty of this for a really long time, so no judgment here, but I do want to share with you what I learned.

The superficial chasing of the perfect guy is a distraction. It is something bright and shiny to pin your focus on that will keep you content for a while. No relationship can survive the hot and heavy thrill of the chase indefinitely. What typically happens is, when the feelings start to wane or settle into something a little less passionate and all-consuming, you will move on to chase the next bright and shiny thing. The underlying issue is you need to address the unhealthy behaviors and thinking that pushes you to jump from one hot thing right into the next.

It's easy to become a passion chaser, fueled by that tear your clothes off, all-consuming, hot need to have naked skin on skin contact with another human. I think it's one of the best feelings out there, and chances are a fair amount of people reading this also think that. You *can* have that kind of passion inside a healthy relationship. In fact, I will venture to say that, inside a healthy relationship, you can have even more passion because there is more trust and more freedom to express yourself without judgment, without worry that getting what you want will make him take away his love.

I had a need to be needed, and so I sought out a partner when I didn't have one, needing to fulfill that need. I wanted passion in my life again, and I thought that came with a man. It didn't, but it took me a really long time to see that. I had to learn to light my own flame and find my own passions without depending on someone else to bring those into my life. I was hardheaded and old-fashioned and thought the right guy would ignite everything for me, so I chased relationships. One after another, as soon as one light faded, I'd end it and move on, swiping left at the next candidate. It was exciting at first, and then I just got tired. Tired of getting my hopes up and putting on heels and makeup. Tired of going on first dates all nervous and jittery. I knew there had to be something more.

Just like the heroin junkies I watched on *Intervention*, I hit my rock bottom. I was tired of things not working out. I was tired of the emptiness I felt. The next relationship wasn't going to make me happy because *I* wasn't happy. I had to fix myself. I had to detox from the things that were keeping me stuck in the patterns that didn't serve me anymore. I sent myself to rehab—a six-month exercise called being alone. I had tried it many times before but always went right back out, looking for my quick fix, only to complete this unsatisfying pattern yet again. I always found myself making promises, saying and doing things I didn't want to do in order to get another hit. Changing who I was and what I wanted and needed to keep the high going as long as possible. Eventually, it would always crash and burn, and I'd be right back out there, hocking my wares to the next guy, desperate for another buzz.

I was good at dating, and I met some really awesome guys during this time. But I still morphed who I was to fit what I thought they wanted. If I had solidified myself more, had stood strong in the confidence of who I was, unwilling to change on the big things, this process would have been so much less painful and lengthy. When I finally stopped rushing back out there to find the right guy and get my next fix, that is when things started to change.

You need to not need it. I know this seems silly and basic, but it is the truth. When you break the addiction to relationships, you free yourself from all the neediness in order to find a healthy one. You will find the right one when you *want* him, but you don't *need* him.

If you are in a healthy relationship and feel the pull of relationship addiction calling, the best thing you can do is work on giving yourself the things that make you happy. Add adventure and excitement into your life and your partnership by doing something new together, or doing "it" somewhere new. The attention you crave from other men is a cry to heal the part of yourself that craves being valued and wanted. Do not rely on men to give this to you. Instead, find ways to increase your self-worth. Healthy relationships have good and bad days. Things wane from time to time when life happens, and this is completely normal. When this happens, never look outside your healthy relationship for the fix. Instead, turn toward your partner. Find something small or fun you can do to add that thrilling newness again. Take a break and play together in whatever way floats your boat.

The Big Takeaway Question: Do you have relationship addiction?

The first step is admitting it and seeing your behavior clearly. If the answer is yes, take some time off from dating. If you are between relationships, take time to heal and refocus on yourself. Don't rush back out there in your quest to find the perfect one. Do a relationship detox.

I was the worst at this because I felt like I was wasting

time. It is not wasting time to work on yourself. Ever. Instead of primping and polishing up for the next round of first dates, date yourself. Take yourself to the movies and buy yourself overpriced snacks. If you have really big balls, go on vacation solo. Fall in love with yourself first.

JUST NO! AND ABUSERS

There's a list of Just No Partners that should be avoided at all costs.

Active Addicts
Active Alcoholics
Recovering Addicts and Alcoholics with less than 5 years of sobriety
Child abusers
Sex Offenders
People who hurt animals
People with a history of domestic violence
People with anger issues

Having lived with an addict, even addicts in recovery are red flags for me. It is too easy to shift into the codependent dynamic with an addict in recovery. Addicts relapse. You will need to decide what is right for you, but I would definitely advise against it. In general, the odds in this situation are never in your favor.

Abusers are never okay. You likely know about sexual abuse and physical abuse, but there are other types to consider, including emotional, psychological abuse, financial abuse, and cultural or identity abuse. So many of these fly under the radar because there is no physical evidence of the abuse and because of a basic misunderstanding of the word abuse. People misclassify it all the time. "But it's not like he hits me," is one phrase I have heard and have used personally as an excuse to stay in an abusive and dysfunctional relationship.

The criteria of physical harm needs to stop being the measuring stick used to define abuse. Abuse is being belittled, being made to feel like you are crazy, being gaslighted, being controlled in any way. Any person who uses fear or tactics to control is an abuser and must be avoided. A healthy man doesn't need to control his partner. Underlying insecurities cause abusers to act out in a myriad of unhealthy ways. This is work that they must undertake before they would ever be partnership material. Abusers are generally amazing excuse-makers and incredible debaters who have an ability to warp circumstances in their minds. They will find endless ways to justify their destructive behaviors.

Abuse can be as simple as using words to make you feel insignificant, dirty, worthless, or ugly. It can be not giving you access to the joint checking account or requiring you to sign over all of your checks without any access to the money. It can be pressuring you to stop working and stay at home and putting you on an allowance to control you. Any act that makes you feel bad about yourself, lowers your self-esteem, or makes you feel isolated, ashamed, afraid, or less than is a form of abuse. Playing mind games, telling you that you are crazy, humiliating you in front of friends and family, these are all forms of abuse. Threatening to leave you or report you to the police, or that he will commit suicide if you do not behave a certain way are forms of abuse. Intimidation, breaking property, displaying weapons, all of these are forms of abuse. Anyone who threatens to out your sexuality or makes racial slurs is abusive. Keeping you in isolation is a form of abuse.

Abusers are very cunning and likable people at first. It can be very difficult to classify an abuser early on, and that is what really stealthy abusers depend on. At first, the all-consuming love bubble makes you feel wanted and needed. Abusers are amazing at spinning the truth. They may approach it as, "I want to take care of you. I am old-fashioned." The first controlling behaviors can be explained away easily, and you might find yourself making excuses. But over time, these traits will become harder to accept, and you will figure out the real root of these is that this person is unhealthy and abusive. Abusers are good at instilling fear and intimidating you into allowing the abuse to continue. It's even harder when it becomes an infatuation abuse, where they demand to be the only person in your life and force you to shut out the rest of the world, closing yourself off from all of your other relationships, like family and close friends.

Love does not make you feel like this. Healthy partners will go out of their way to prevent their partner from feeling any of these emotions. A healthy partner will never twist the truth, lie, or control you to obtain their selfish outcome. A healthy partner will always look for ways to support you and care for your heart.

All of the negative emotions talked about above have no place in a healthy relationship. You must develop a zero-tolerance policy to abuse. You do not deserve to live in fear and intimidation that crushes the joy out of life. You deserve a partner who protects you, who pours love on you and wants to see you thrive and succeed both on your own and with him. Love wants you to develop your entire being, which includes friendships and family relationships. Love wants to give you the freedom to chase your dreams wherever they may lead and will never shame you for trying, even when you fail. Love is connection and support. Abuse chokes all of the love out of your life.

If you are in an abusive relationship, please find a way out. Make a plan, reach out for support and encouragement, and most of all be safe. There are a lot of unhealthy people out there searching for their next victim to control. Do not let it be you. If you have made a mistake and gotten involved with an abuser, do not beat yourself up. Simply make a plan and execute it. I think the less the abuser knows about it the better. I have seen too many sad stories on the news about women who were murdered when their sick partner was told they were leaving. You must protect yourself and let a fully vetted, trusted person in on your plan. Keep your cards close to your chest, and do yourself a favor and leave that behind.

You deserve to live in a place where you feel supported and loved, where your heart is protected and you are allowed to grow more fully into your gifts and the truth of who you are. You should not feel any shame, ever, for wanting what you want. There is nothing you can desire in life that is wrong. Do not give someone that kind of power in your life. You have earned this right by being born. You owe nothing. If you cannot get the kind of support and love you need inside your relationship, then cut yourself free and learn how to give that to yourself.

The Big Takeaway Question: Is my relationship healthy or abusive?

This is one of the hardest things I will ask you to do in

this book. But if you find yourself in an unhappy and sad place of being controlled and manipulated, know that you are strong enough to pull yourself together and cut yourself free. Look with fresh eyes at the reality of how your partner treats you.

LOVE IS...

The fairytales lied, and your parents were assholes for reading them to you. They set you up for failure, to want the wrong things, and to expect that woodland animals are gifted seamstresses. Sleeping Beauty, Snow White, Rapunzel—all drama filled circuses with the main storyline being that you must wait for the man to come and save you and that his kiss will bring you back to life. These stories are told to little girls as examples of love, and they buy into them because they are young and impressionable and because trustworthy adults are reading the stories to them.

Love is everything. Love is all you need. Love makes the world go round. All these cute catchphrases fan the flame. But you can't help yourself because you are wired to love. All humans are. It is a need that, as infants, if it is stifled, stunts your growth. Like food, water, and shelter, without love, human beings perish a long painful death. Love is the simplistic cure for everything—racism, homophobia, depression, school shootings. All the problems our modern world has today could be solved with a heaping dose of it, but it seems to be a scarce natural resource sometimes. Like the morel mushrooms you hunt in the springtime in Iowa, sometimes you are lucky and hit the motherlode, and sometimes you walk through the damp underbrush and find nothing.

So, it makes perfect sense that you desire it because, as part of the human race, you can be insanely different from all the other people on the planet, except for this one truth. You are driven to love and be loved. If you stripped everything else away, it is the one central value that guides all of us. No one is exempt from this. Not you, not me.

The need for love will drive you to do things that are out of character. To move across the country, to go on a blind date, to try to change who you are to fit the person you are with. Your want to be loved can crowd out all your common sense and decision-making abilities. It's a powerful force that people will do nearly anything in their quest to keep it. This is dangerous because you will sacrifice things you shouldn't sacrifice. You will warp to change and hide parts of yourself to hold on to its fleeting high.

There are two kinds of love, the kind that builds and the kind that destroys. The kind that builds is softer and sweeter. It progresses at a smooth natural clip. It flows and is warmth personified. It is ease and light and peace.

The other kind is the fire. It is passionate and destructive. It consumes everything quickly and burns out fast. It is the rollercoaster ride with the highest highs and the lowest lows that leave you breathless and terrified, yet wanting to ride it one more time.

The difference is so vast. Real, true, abiding love is the first kind. It is a gentle unlocking of your soul. The sweetest shift that resonates so deep inside it will make you gasp in wonder. Your eyes will be opened wider. Where once you had blinders on, you can now see everything so clearly. Every little detail is crisp and sharp and lusciously colored like when you go from a pixelated cabinet style TV to the stunning color and quality of 4000K, or when I opened my eyes after LASIK surgery and a whole new world greeted my freshly lasered corneas.

The other kind is sadly more sought after, the lusty, passionate, all-consuming desire you are taught to chase. You are told that if you aren't experiencing the heart palpitations, there isn't a spark. While a degree of this is true, there definitely has to be a physical element and a passionate element, society has you focus on this part too intently. As a result, you might overlook a slow burn style of love that is right under your nose.

Lasting love ebbs and flows. Some days it's passionate and sexy. Some days it's working through your own insecurities. Some days it's barely speaking and then calling a cease-fire and cooking together. It is building a life that fulfills two completely different people, and this is messy stuff. It isn't all easy street. Some days it's work. If you are ready to love, you are ready to work. You are ready to open yourself, even the parts of yourself that you try to hide. You are ready to compromise, not settle. There is a succinct difference. Compromise does not ask you to go against your own values and needs. Compromise is conceding on your wants in favor of the relationship.

Lasting love invites you to continue on your journey of self-discovery, but now you'll have a cheering section. It encourages you to continue to walk your path of truth and to uncover more authentic bits of yourself to share with someone else. Healthy love is two complete people bringing the best of themselves to the other to share the overflow.

The Big Takeaway Question: What kind of love have you chased in the past?

Total compassionate honesty is necessary. Look at your past relationships and identify your patterns. Classify if they were healthy or unhealthy.

YOU ARE THE PROBLEM, BUT YOU ARE ALSO THE SOLUTION

All the good ones are gone.
Dating in your forties is like trying to find the least smelly and damaged thing at the thrift store.
Good men are hard to find.
All guys want is a hook-up.

I could go on and on, right? But these are just a few of the myths women tell themselves when they are thrust back out into the dating realm after a break-up, divorce, or other life-altering change. There is a very difficult truth I want to share with you. The biggest reason you can't find the relationship you want is you. Your preconceived ideas and false beliefs, your weakened standards and general wishy-washiness of not knowing what you want, or settling for less than you deserve.

The good news is that even though you are the problem, you are also the solution. Right now, you can undertake the most important work of your life to fix yourself. It will have the most impact of any other work you ever do. It will spill out onto every relationship, not just the romantic ones, but in the relationships with your kids, the ones at work. Every relationship you currently have will be deeper and richer as a result of the inner work you do to get out of your own way.

I've spent thousands of dollars on therapy and books, looking for the fast track to healing. I know this will hurt to hear, but there isn't one. The only thing that works is time, self-compassion, and filling your brain and soul with the good things so that your cup of goodness overflows. It takes an honest eye to look into your life and see with a bit of detachment what is truly not working and what part you have played in the dysfunction. This is hard. It will test your inner strength. It will force you to grow and forge your new patterns if you embrace it and let it.

Instead of looking outside yourself for the next dopamine hit that comes with a six-pack and dimples to make you happy, you need to stay in your own lane and do things that make you happy. Like attracts like. Happy attracts happy.

You have to change the way you talk to yourself and the limiting and false beliefs that you convince yourself are truths. Every day, your brain scans your world for evidence that confirms what you believe. If you believe all men suck, that there aren't any good ones left, then that is what you will find. Evidence to support that belief will come forward, and you will confirm your own suspicions. But the reverse is also true. If you believe that, in a world of seven and a half billion people, there might be one, possibly one person, that might be a decent healthy human to interact with, then that is what you will find.

I dated a lot after my divorce, and almost every man I met was solid, happy, and interesting. I believed that there were still amazing people in the dating pool, who, just like me, had either made a terrible mistake the first time out of the gate, or who had been widowed, or just weren't on the get married at twenty track like everyone else. Because I believed this, that is what I found, and I had a lot of fun meeting some really impressive men.

The first step to finding a healthy guy is to take a look at your limiting beliefs. You have to do a deep dig into your own negative thoughts about the dating process, your skepticism, your fears, and your worries. Stop inviting these into your dating life. Re-write all of the thoughts in your head about scarcity and lack into abundance and availability. There are good people out there looking to connect with other good people. I promise you. If you don't believe this right now, you need to address that pattern of thinking. Your own misconceptions are getting in the way of them finding you. Those untrue thoughts dim your light so it doesn't shine as bright.

The Big Takeaway Question: What misconceptions about dating do you believe that are getting in your way?

The easiest way to find them is to identify things that make you feel the bad emotions—skeptical, paranoid, combative. When you think about men or being in a relationship with someone, what negatives come up for you? Re-write these as positives and fill your mind with them.

DADDY ISSUES

The media loves to tell you that daddy issues are the root of most unhealthy relationships, and while I do agree there is some truth to that, I think it goes a little deeper. Unconsciously, I believe you are looking for qualities in a partner that your dad had, and the reason you do that is because it's familiar. It is what you are used to, and your mind looks to complete that pattern. That's why all therapists will ask you about your core family relationships. A lot of the trauma and bad thinking developed from there.

My dad was a great dad, but when he was laid off, he had to take a traveling salesman job to support our family. This meant being on the road nearly seven days a week, getting up before we woke up and coming home after we were asleep. He wasn't around much, and I never got to experience that fatherly love that teaches a teenage girl (one of the most skittish and impressionable things on the planet) what she should expect from male energy.

It left me needy, like a puppy dog following boys around and lapping up any little morsel of affection. I don't blame him because the man had seven mouths to feed. Seven! The idea of that gives me heart palpitations when I remember how hard it has been in the past for me to feed less than half of that. He did his best. When he was home, he truly tried to spend quality time with us, whether it was playing the basketball game horse in the driveway, a marathon game of Monopoly in the basement during a blizzard, or helping me learn how to wood burn on the Papa Smurf shape he cut out one day for me on his band saw. He definitely tried, but it wasn't enough. I was starved, so starved for positive attention from any male that anything would do.

This lowers your bar, just a smidge, every day. It seems small at first, but over time, the bar becomes so low that the barrier to entry is nearly non-existent and anyone can take a quick step over it. This shift happens around fifteen, which for most girls is the worst possible time. Raging hormones and physical changes are at war already in your body, making you lose your mind at the tiniest infraction, and soothing yourself with a copious amount of chocolate and salt. It's not your fault that these incredibly hard to understand and difficult dynamics are given to you without explanation or education. You just have to learn as you go and do the best you can.

The lucky girls have an amazing foundation in place from a father who loved them the right ways, who took the time to teach them what a real man should do, be, and how he should treat a woman. The others of you have gaping knowledge gaps, sometimes huge bottomless chasms of nothingness that you are forced to scale. And because you are immature, your methods of scaling these chasms are shifty and shitty at best. You muddle through doing the best you can, with the limited skills you have available.

I wish all fathers understood the power they had over their daughters. I wish, as a society, we valued fathers more and encouraged their strength. I wish we celebrated their influence on more days than just Father's Day. I wish we gave them the accolades they deserve in our society. God is a father, and we have slowly minimized his influence in our society, just like we have minimized every other father figure in our modern culture.

A good dad is a rock, a source of support, love, security, and safety for his children. Without that sense of safety, you are endlessly drifting, always searching for it, but unable to find it. The best dads give their daughters childhoods they don't need to recover from. A real dad's first renovation project is to install the bar to which his daughter compares every future male relationship against. They understand the gold standard of relationships starts with them and set the bar very high for potential mates.

How do you recover from daddy issues and prevent them from being spilled over onto your new relationships? The only real way is to find those things for yourself—the safety, the security, the inner strength. Still looking for them outside of yourself is a recipe for disaster because you will become a bottomless pit of neediness and wear your partner out. It is not their responsibility to give that to you. It is not their job to fill you up. In the early stages of a relationship, when things are sweetie pie this and love muffin that, they will bend over backward to give you anything you need. But long-term, this strategy will never work. You will exhaust them and yourself with the constant need.

You don't get to pick your parents. You are born into a family, and you learn your lessons from them, good or bad. But you *do* get to pick your partners, and that is where the blame shifts from your dad's shoulders to yours. You are the one responsible for breaking the cycle of it or choosing to continue it.

It is your job to fill you up. It is your job to calm the fear in your heart and fill it with the things you need to feel safe and strong. Just because you have daddy issues doesn't mean you are destined to have crappy relationships for the rest of your life. It just means you need to do the internal work *before* you put yourself out there. You need to fix yourself first.

The Big Takeaway Question: What was your relationship with your dad like?

This may be a painful exercise, but it is so important. Identify how your father or lack of a father shaped your thinking about love and men. Can you tie events of your previous relationships together with this new understanding?

HEAL? WHAT DO YOU KNOW?

People will tell you to take time for yourself and heal after a break-up. I think I even heard an equation once about the number of years you spent together should be multiplied in months or some shit. When I got divorced, I wasn't hearing any of it. I was a dumbass.

You don't know me. I have been grieving this marriage for years inside it. Now that I am free, I want to cut loose and right some wrongs!

I wanted fun, I wanted excitement, and I wanted the butterflies that came with being in love. I mean, who doesn't? As a result, I was out there downloading dating apps just a few months after the end of my marriage. I had some nice fun times and gained fond dirty memories that will keep me happy in the nursing home someday, but then I had a painful string of relationships that scarred me and my kids for a few years following, which could have completely been avoided.

I vividly remember talking to my best friend, and she said, "Now that the divorce is over, you can all heal." At the time, I thought, "Heal? I don't need to heal. Getting out of this relationship is healing. I am ready for the next great love of my life." I was hardheaded and stupid and paid the price for years. I was always trying to figure out who I was and what I wanted inside a relationship. I went from one to the next, attracting unhealthy partners because I was so unhealthy.

I didn't want to take the time to heal because I had wasted so much time already. Sixteen years inside the wrong relationship. Now, the hair was graying and my hips were widening as they marched toward menopause, and I thought, *I have got to prove to myself that I can be in a good marriage. Now! The old girl ain't getting any younger.* So, I caved to the panic that comes when your time clock is nearing the end of double overtime with five seconds on the shot clock. Now, I see the shot clock was stupid. Why did I put that kind of pressure on myself? Throwing up hail Marys fast and furious, sometimes bricks off the backboard, sometimes complete airballs. To keep going with the basketball analogy, I needed to take a time out. Take a breath and reassess what was working and what wasn't working.

I didn't take that time out until the break-up of my engagement. After that relationship was over, I gathered up the shattered pieces of my heart and said enough was enough. Finally, I took myself to the movies, alone. I started pursuing my own career path, and I worked to finally figure out what I wanted. I read and I journaled and I wrote a list of the qualities I was looking for in a perfect partner. I never stopped believing that one day I would find someone who would fit into my life so perfectly, but first I had to get clear and define the kind of life I wanted to live. But even more important, I had to take the time to heal my brokenness because it kept getting in the way. I avoided it like the mess you sweep into the closet when company comes over, but it was always there, waiting. I finally took the time to clean up the mess that was me.

Being really goal-oriented, I also made goals for myself. I was painting a very clear picture of what I wanted my life to look like, and for the first time, not taking into account anyone else's ideas, wants, or needs. It was simply me. What kind of life did I want to live? What did it look like? What feelings did I want to feel? What could I get really excited about in terms of where I would live and where I would travel, and what would I do? In the early mornings, ramped up on dark roast coffee that was so strong you could almost chew it, I dreamed and fantasized about the life I wanted to live, and it became so real, I felt I could dream it into existence.

I traveled to Florida and to New Orleans with my sister and a couple of close girlfriends, and I traveled to Scotland, truly the most beautiful place I have ever been to. In Scotland, I healed so much of my broken heart, letting go of pain from the loss of my mom, the struggles with my son, and the ugly relationships I had engaged in. Scotland was a full reset for me, a trip I always dreamed about taking since I first read *Eat, Pray, Love*. You don't need to travel to Europe to heal, but if you can carve out time for yourself in a natural setting, it can be incredibly cathartic. Being in nature and forest bathing will heal your soul like nothing else can. It is a gift you can give yourself.

Taking the time to heal is also a gift you can give yourself. Time spent healing is not wasted time. Time reflecting and digging deep into the unique problems you face is not for naught. It is some of the most important work you will ever undertake if you want to be happy. How can you figure out who is the right partner if you don't know yourself intimately first? Discover the things that excite you, then breathe life back into your life and chase them. If you don't know where to begin, just invite curiosity into your life.

How do you know when you are done healing? It's a

feeling of contentment. A knowing that you will be okay no matter what. An understanding that love is incredible and although you would welcome it into your life, you don't *need* it. Everything you need is inside you already. If you can't say that, you aren't ready. Trying to do this kind of work inside a relationship is very difficult. It takes longer because you are distracted by love and because love asks you to enter into agreements with another person. If you don't know who you are at your core, what your values are, and what is most important in your life without a man, then it is even murkier to figure it out with one. It is a recipe for disaster because you will be inclined to compromise on things that you shouldn't.

I was an idiot, and if I had taken the time to heal years before, I would have avoided so much pain, for myself and for my kids. But I love to learn lessons the hard way, so the painful route was the road I was on. Eventually, I got off the struggle bus and took the time to heal, and that made all the difference. The relationship that I got into after that healing period was 'the one' and he is the perfect partner for me. Not a perfect partner, because no one is. But he is the perfect partner *for me*. The quiet time to heal paid off.

The Big Takeaway Question: Have you truly taken the time off to heal?

If you have not, there is no time like the present to put yourself first, to do the things that heal your heart, and to get out into the forest or the ocean. Nature is incredibly healing. If you haven't taken the time off to heal, why not?

WHY BEING A CHAMELEON DOES NOT SERVE YOU

I'm a really easy person to get along with, on purpose. I was taught to be a giver, to make things easier and sacrifice for others, to never be selfish. These values were ingrained in me since birth. While I believe that to a degree these qualities can be good, the reverse is also true. Overgiving, being a martyr, and always smoothing the path for others is the fast train to Passive Agressiveville, which was my favorite vacation destination for many, many years.

These qualities spilled over into my adult life for the first four decades. When asked, "What do you want to do?" I'd automatically reply, "I don't know. What do you want to do?" And then I would live with whatever the other person decided. I did, however, learn a lesson from a very nice guy I had the good fortune to date for a short time. I was so happy with myself because I had finally attracted a solid, successful guy and tricked him into wanting to date me more than once. Our second date was an impromptu late-night date, and he asked me the dreaded question, "What do you want to do?"

This back and forth happened for the next several painful

minutes. "I don't know," I'd say coyly. "What do you feel like? I don't care, I'm easy." When asked if I wanted to see the latest Avengers movie, I said, "If you want to," when I would rather stick needles in my eyes.

He was exasperated, and I heard it in his voice. He finally decided we should grab dinner because it was a second date and movies are not a good way to get to know someone better. As I breathed a sigh of relief that I wouldn't have to try to stay awake through a superhero movie, I knew for a fact, my wishy-washy, going with the flow even if I hated it, was what did us in. I know this for a fact because he told me later.

A successful man is looking for an equal—someone who has an opinion, someone who can make a decision. Waffling back and forth is about as sexy as granny panties. A successful man is likely tired of having to make decisions all day long at work, so he wants to come home and for things to be easy. He wants to be able to relax, not dive into more negotiations with his partner. A man would love nothing more than exact directions on how to please you in the most effective way possible, in the bedroom and out of it. Seriously.

You know what is a turn on? A woman who is passionate about something. A woman who is excited and happy with stories to tell about why these things mean so much. A woman who can answer the question as old as time. Where should we go to dinner?

You know what is sexy? A woman with an opinion. A woman who knows what she likes. A woman who orders more than a salad at dinner. Can you go to the other extreme? Yes! Don't be the demanding and hard to please bitch either. Life is about balance. Have an opinion, but be flexible.

Instead of morphing and shapeshifting to fit the man you

are interested in by pretending to like the same things, be more of who you are. Be confident in the things you love and want in your life. Don't compromise who you are in order to land a man. This might be temporarily successful, but you will never be in the right relationship where you are unabashedly yourself and loved for being so. When you make concessions to fit the mold of what someone else wants, you compromise the truth of you. Something that you should never compromise. The real true you, the beautiful bumpy soul you are, is perfect as it is. Your weirdo is out there, the one who's heart syncs up with yours. Believe it.

The bible backs me up. God makes pairs. He loaded them on the arc to save civilization from the flood. Hello, Adam and Eve? There is a perfectly imperfect weirdo out there looking for you right now. But when you change who you are or present yourself in a manner that isn't consistent with your true self, he will never find you. He might be looking at you right now and decide you aren't it by the masks you're wearing.

The older you are, the more confidence you should have in the person that you have become. You are more comfortable putting that girl out there because you aren't as stuck in the high school world of fitting in anymore. You might have fought some battles that have given you the confidence to step into the truth of you. That is a good place to be. I wish every woman had the confidence to do that.

If you don't yet know what you love, then date yourself. It sounds super cheesy, but it is effective. Try the new Asian place with the egg rolls people can't stop talking about. Figure out your body and what gets your motor running. Am I taking about masturbation? Yes! You can't give good directions until you know how to get there yourself. Take an art class, a dance class, or buy a bicycle and ride with a group you find on Facebook. Discover who you are and do more of what makes you happy. Happy girls are instantly a thousand percent more attractive and fun to be around.

Figure out who you are and let that freak flag fly. Don't hide it. Trot that fucker out like you are at the Macy's Thanksgiving Day Parade. Dance around with it, and you will be surprised by the compatibility of the men you will attract.

The Big Takeaway Question: What ways have you compromised yourself in the past to fit the person you were dating?

This is a difficult truth to acknowledge, but when you do, it can set you free. Journal about the times you have adapted to fit in when you went along to get along. Then also make a list of you. Who you are, the things you love, what qualities you embody, and find more ways to add to this list. Embrace these qualities and put them on display. They will be a beacon for your weirdo.

GAMES ARE FOR CHILDREN AND PARTIES

Hearts are fragile things, filled with emotions and vulnerability, and that is why playing games hurts. The stakes are immeasurably high, and there are so many expectations and high hopes. Emotionally immature people play games, but healthy people don't set out to manipulate and hurt others or approach relationships as a game to play. Both men and women are guilty of this, mostly because they are afraid to reveal who they truly are. It is easier to play hide and seek and to build walls. Because when you cut through all the bullshit and reveal your true self, the possibility of someone rejecting who you are at your core is terrifying.

So, instead, you hide and only show bits and pieces of yourself to avoid possible rejection. You drop hints at what you want, hoping he will get it and understand and then be able to decode your emotions and give you what you want, but it doesn't work that way. All that does is drag out the inevitable. It takes longer for people to decide if it is a good fit because you are a championship poker player who's unwilling to show your hand.

There is a better way, and it is indeed terrifying. First,

there is the getting to know you stage in a new relationship, where you try to find connections on basic trivial things, like hobbies, and see if you have the same values. If they make it to round two, then you need to reveal more of your deeper authentic self. Most of the time, relationships jump to straight intimacy and then try to bounce back into the discovery option. Why is it easier to be physically intimate with someone than to have a real talk about your real vulnerabilities?

Healthy relationships have consistency. You won't be afraid to speak your truth, and you will be able to discern if who you are aligns with your partner. The best way to do this is to be direct. Talk about the important things and be very clear about what you need from a partner. Drop the masks and the want to please. Say what you mean and mean what you say. Clarity is important. If you find yourself unwilling or unable to do this, then you are not ready. You have more interior work to do.

When you make compromises against important values, it will keep you in the wrong relationship longer. It will have you frittering and toiling away with the wrong partner, wasting more of your time and theirs. When you play games, you will frustrate your potential partner. Men appreciate directness. They like to be told the truth in as few words as possible and under control. If you are an overemotional powerhouse, it will be hard for someone to take you seriously. Sometimes, you need time to understand and digest why you feel a certain way about a situation. Look underneath the emotions of fear and anger to find what the real cause is and then find the best way to articulate this to your partner.

Dropping hints and expecting him to get it never works. The best way to handle it is by being honest about your soft spots. You know what hurts you or triggers you to act out in a certain way. For instance, I had to say to my guy, "There is so much pain surrounding my son, so when something happens with him, it spins me out and I am very touchy about it. The best way you can support me is with hugs and empathy. Don't try to fix it. I need to fix how I respond to the stress of that relationship. I just want you to be there for me. You don't have to do anything to fix it or come up with a solution. I have that part handled. Just be there for me. Take me out and get my mind off of it. Give me a massage or a hug."

Telling someone honestly what hurts and how they can support you is an act of love. It allows you to have a bad day and still be supported. It shows you are mature and working through life's problems, instead of stomping around in a bad mood or withdrawing when he throws out sarcastic comments. Telling him exactly what he can do will be the most direct path to happiness in your relationship. Stop the relationship draining guessing games and passive-aggressive contests. Cut right to the heart of the matter. Sometimes you don't know what the heart of the matter is. That is okay, too. Just tell the other person, "I am struggling with this right now. I need a little time to process it and figure it out."

You know the cave talked about in *Men are From Mars and Women are from Venus?* That when a man is struggling with a problem, they retreat to their cave to figure it out. It is a legit thing. When my guy is struggling with something, whether it be an issue at work or in our relationship, he disconnects. Early on, I noticed a pattern that would scare me and spin me out. I wasn't healthy enough to see what part I played in it quite yet, but I knew that when he withdrew, I worried there was something wrong with me. I internalized every time he went into the cave as that being the end of our relationship. Finally, through a heart to heart talk, I was able to say to him, "Just tell me you have something on your mind and need some space. That, I can understand. Don't go and hide. Tell me you are going to go and hide and what is making you want to do it in the first place. That is something that I can accept."

I know he will eventually come back out and get back on track with me. He needs to be able to do that from time to time and not feel guilty about it. And, at the same time, I need to be able to understand what is happening, allow him the space he needs, and not sit in anxiety about it. This took a couple of really clear conversations. I had to learn to use "I feel" statements, but this was a breakthrough in our relationship. He also said something really clear and healing to me personally that I want to share. He said, "Of course, we are alright. We will always be alright." That calmed my little anxious heart more than anything. I knew without a doubt that he was in it for the long haul. Whatever came up, we could face it together. That I could trust him when he had to go to the cave. It was an amazing breakthrough for me personally and one of the reasons I love him so deeply.

The Big Takeaway Question: Do you play games in your relationships?

Really look at this and journal about the ways you have played games in the past. What would have been a clearer path to a solution? What were you afraid to say and why? What makes you want to play games in the first place? What games did others play with you? How did that make you feel?

THE MYTH OF THE ONE THAT GOT AWAY

Songs are written about it, poems and movies use it as a storyline, and I used to believe this was a truth. This myth that there is one person destined to be yours. Like a pair of shoes, you are compelled to search the earth for your mate until you find them. I bought into the lie that there was one and only one that was perfect for me. I eventually discovered this was another romantic lie.

There is no one that got away because, for whatever reason, fundamentally, you and this person did not work. It wasn't a case of wrong place, wrong time. It was firmly a case of the wrong person. Timing is not everything. If it doesn't work, he's not the right one. Period.

The romantic part of me used to say, "The stars did not align for us, but maybe someday they will." I had a relationship like this and stayed steeped in regret after walking away from it for nearly two years. I called him the one that got away. I would bore my girlfriends to tears over copious amounts of margaritas and salsa, sobbing on their weary shoulders that I would never love another. They rolled their eyes (I don't blame them, I have a flair for the dramatic.) and told me there are plenty of men out there. I would lament that this was not the case and mentally bash my head against the wall of regret, keeping part of my heart imprisoned and unavailable.

I collect quotes. I have a Pinterest board filled with them because sometimes you just need the right turn of phrase to sear hope into your soul. One that has brought me immense comfort is "Whatever is meant for me cannot miss me, and whatever misses me is not meant for me."

If you could just blindly trust God or the Universe, you will see that the right person or opportunity appears right when you need it and right when you are ready for it and not a second before. There is no such thing as missing out on the love of your life, because if it doesn't work out, then that wasn't the love of your life.

Regret is hard to live with because it will lie to you. In your mind, you will place far more emphasis on the good and prefer to leave the bad in the dark. This disproportionate way of rehashing the greatest hits reel from the one that got away while tears stream down your face and you eat your feelings is another lie you tell yourself. There will never be another man who loves me like he did. I miss him. I am resolved to live the rest of my life loveless and brokenhearted. It is time I accept this universal truth. Wrong!

In reality, men truly are like buses. If you wait long enough another one will come, like clockwork. There is no "the one," so you can stop beating yourself up right now for letting go of that almost perfect man. You can stop rationalizing the things you miss in an effort to talk yourself into rekindling the relationship. It wasn't enough, it didn't work, so the best thing you can do is walk away and find something new, something better, or continue to work on yourself so you are completely clear on what you are looking for while you wait.

It is easy to paint the picture of a false reality while still dreamy-eyed for the one that got away. If he was the one, he wouldn't have gotten away. The right one sticks. No matter what. The right one is ready and willing and will do anything it takes to keep you by his side. So, if he got away, do yourself a favor and let that man go. Continuing to hold on to the memories and reminiscing will only serve to make this harder. Quit lying to yourself and accept that he wasn't the right guy, and you are one step closer to recognizing what you do want. You are closer to being able to identify the qualities you are looking for in your perfect mate, so that when he shows up in front of you, you will know.

Pining after the one that got away is dangerous because you're looking at the relationship with your love goggles on and focusing on the past. Loneliness can drive you to do things that aren't in your best interest. It can keep you attached to the past, occupied slightly so that your heart isn't open or ready. Love will evade and elude you in this state. You can't move forward with open arms and find the one that fits you better if you are still attached to the one that wasn't quite right.

Relationships that are on-again and off-again should be switched to the permanently off position. This is coming from a woman who was engaged twice to the same man and wasted the better part of three years figuring out he was not the right guy. Getting back together with your ex will assuage your loneliness temporarily, but the old issues will come raging back eventually. You deserve peace in your relationship, not manufactured drama and twists at every turn that cause you to sit in anxiety.

Let the one that got away go. Fully. Wish them well, thank them for the lessons they taught you, and move forward with the knowledge that your next bus is right around the corner. Take a breath, open your heart, and wait. It will come.

The Big Takeaway Question: Are you stuck in regret? Are you engaged in on-again, off-again relationships?

Take a close look at your exes and the way you think about them. If you are pining for one, take the time to cut yourself free.

THE DRAMA MAMA

Our world is filled with drama. You can seek it out on Netflix, social media, or through the latest neighborhood gossip. Everyone loves a great story, and that's natural. As human beings, it is normal to crave excitement. If you are used to relationships where you're fighting then fucking, you will struggle to find a good one that will withstand the rollercoaster ride, and you are likely addicted to the drama. One of the most enlightening things my therapist ever said to me was, "You are going to have to get used to boredom and quiet. You've been living this high-stakes, drama-filled life for so long that your new normal is chaos. It is going to be hard for you to not seek it out." At first, I was like, "What? You don't know me! I want peace and comfort and ease. I am in *therapy*."

But taking a closer look at my life, at the self-sabotaging patterns that were so ingrained in me and how they manifested in the partners I chose, it was obvious that she was right. That one truth she shared set me free, as soon as I was able to accept it. The truth hurts, and that was a difficult one to swallow. By understanding that, instead of thinking things were happening *to* me, I was forced to acknowledge my own active participation in the circus I was currently living.

I'm a writer. I love stories, dramadies especially, the ones that rip your heart out and have your pulse pounding with a side of funny. Unfortunately, this is not the right mindset for successful long-term relationships. Admitting my own love for drama was enlightening, and confronting the truth was a big part of finally figuring things out and fixing myself.

When you can look at your life in a detached away, away from the intensity of emotion, and see it as it really is, this distance will give you the answers you need to make the changes you need to make. Drama isn't necessary to feel alive. Living on bursts of adrenaline and cortisol will burn you up and out. Engaging in drama is like downing energy drinks for your endocrine system. It keeps you firing at a high frequency, whirring and spinning in a high-pitched frenzy, racing toward your eventual burn-out.

A better way is to step away from the drama and reprogram your body and your mind. I have to admit, after being on high alert for a solid four years, it has taken a total reboot to get me back to a somewhat normal state. Operating too high up the drama scale is destructive because, when something comes into your life that is truly worthy of the stress and pain, you will be so far off the drama charts from running high and hot already.

It's like when you have a horrible burn. The skin is very sensitive, and you have to be careful not to disturb it while it heals. You avoid touching it with anything, even water in the shower because it's so painful and inflamed. In this high drama state, even the slightest brush will send you to the stratosphere because you are already running higher than anyone should. Your drama motor is on burn-out, and then all it takes is one small incident to hit the Noz and send you spinning out.

Drama is no fun for anyone. As I have gotten older, it has become easier and easier to rid my life of the drama and people who bring it to me. One at a time, they've got to go. As you get older, you give less fucks about hurting people's feelings and sacrificing your sanity in order to be nice to people you can't stand being around. The easiest way to a drama-free life is to limit the access of the crazy-makers. The ones who thrive on it and bring it to your doorstep. This cleaning of your house will open up spaces for others who energize you and support you. People who you glow around and who bring out the best in you.

It is a useful exercise to carefully consider every relationship in your life and classify if they bring the crazy or the peace. If you can cut out the crazy ones completely, that is a great place to start. If some of them are related to you, possibly even your older or adult children, the process will be more delicate. You will need to set boundaries. You will have to train yourself not to make their drama yours. Just because they are living in a state of chaos doesn't mean that you have to. By letting them live their lives and refusing to get sucked into their crazy-making, you can support them in a healthier way. You can model what healthy detachment looks like and maybe even inspire them to make some changes.

When your kids are involved, this will be incredibly difficult because you will have to fight your natural programming to fix and take care of your young. Over the age of ten, a child needs to develop skills to handle their own lives. You can help by talking them through the problem, listening, and helping guide them to make a healthy decision on how to handle it.

Healthy men hate drama, and even unhealthy ones will claim to hate it all over their dating profiles. A woman who has her shit under control and doesn't bring unnecessary drama to the relationship is much more attractive to any man.

Choosing to live in drama is a choice. You don't have to participate.

The Big Takeaway Question: Who brings drama to your life?

Inventory every relationship in your life. Do they bring drama or peace? If you bring the most drama to your own life, get to the bottom of why you do it. There is always a payoff on behavior that you repeat. Figure out what that payoff is and fix it. Typically, people who crave drama were never seen and accepted as they are. They are desperate for attention, so any kind will do, even the negative kind. If this is you, find healthy ways to be acknowledged in your life.

THE POOP SUITCASE

Most of the time, you push the work of healing yourself off to the side in favor of finding love as soon as possible. The break-up thought process is this: *Sweet Jesus, I'm not getting any younger. I need a distraction. I've wasted so much time with the wrong person, so now I need to find the right one asap. My kids need a father figure.* There is an endless litany of reasons at your fingertips why you pursue love when you know you aren't ready.

It's a different kind of biological clock that makes you crave coupling up because that is what you are used to, but the reality is that you need to stop. Be alone. Fix yourself, or you are bringing your giant suitcase of poop into the next relationship and encouraging your new partner to take a bath in it.

You're welcome for the graphic description, but it's true. You have to wash and dry your own shitty emotional baggage instead of dragging it into the next relationship. You need to strength-train your emotions as much as you strength-train your body while you are at the gym working on your revenge bod. This is hard work. Usually, after a rough break-up or a shitty divorce, you are dying to get right back out there and right some wrongs, not spend time doing the hard work of increasing your emotional health.

The issue with this is that the old problems and issues follow you into the next relationship because the common denominator is you. If you skip the crucial step of understanding and healing and accepting your own brokenness that led to the end of the relationship, you will be doomed to repeat yourself. Over and over, the same issues will come up until you are brave enough and bold enough to work through them. It will be an endless loop of the same thing, but the leading male role will change from time to time. You drag along the unhealed parts of you, stuffed into the poop suitcase, ready to open it up and spring it on the next unknowing victim. Chances are, they are doing the same thing to you with their own brand of bullshit. Will this make for a healthy relationship? Fuck no.

You have to clean up your messes. Yourself. You don't need someone to rescue you or take care of you. You need to summon the resources to do this for yourself. It is backbreaking dirty work, and not the good kind of dirty. One by one, each area of your life should be looked at and addressed so you can bring the bright, shiny, new you to the next relationship. It is hard enough to be in a healthy partnership, so don't kill your chances by dragging your poop suitcase into it. Deal with your own shit.

When you love something and value it, you take care of it. Our neighbor loved his car, maybe more than he loved his wife. He was out in the driveway, lovingly hand washing that thing every four days, slowly rubbing the turtle wax into the hood in swooping circles. It was immaculate. That kind of dedication and maintenance is what is required in your own life. Love yourself to do this important work and you will find that your next relationship is so much easier and has fewer complications because your squeaky-clean heart entered into it.

The Big Takeaway Question: What messes do you need to clean up?

It's not sexy, but this is an important question to ask yourself. Figure out what your messes are and begin to clean them so you can bring your immaculate heart into your next relationship.

GET OUT OF YOUR HEAD

A woman's brain is a fascinating thing. It's where you store everything—your hopes, your dreams, your fears, your memories. It is the epicenter of your world. The problem becomes when your brain is overactive. When your brain is on overdrive and creates false stories and realities, spinning out on things that aren't even the truth.

Overthinking is the fast track to misery. Stop dissecting every text a man sends. Stop decoding his hidden meanings based on his punctuation. Stop gauging his feelings and interest based on how much time passes between texts, or spending hours translating what a particular emoji means. Stop reading and re-reading texts and sending screenshots to your girlfriends. Stop having long chat sessions about what you should text back or if you should be offended. It is an exercise in futility that is the treadmill to hell. It gives you something to do, but it's a total waste of energy. The truth is that men just don't put as much thought into that kind of thing. They don't analyze and agonize over what words they send you. They just don't. They're basic.

It's amazing the imagination a woman has. You can create

entire movies in your head about what a guy thinks of you. How an interaction went, what you should have said, what you should have done. This is another useless waste of your precious time.

Someone who has been traumatized will be especially good at this craziness. You will be in self-protection mode, all over the place, jittery and squirrely, on high alert for signs that he will break your heart. You have work to do there if your brain is consumed by this. If you are spending hours consumed by research and making sure he is not too friendly with other girls, or you're looking at every photo he's posted on Facebook since 2005, you need to refocus.

If you read into every word and dissect his texts and mood on a daily basis, you are in your head too much and it is destructive. You are either in a volatile, unhealthy relationship that you need to leave, or you need to heal the part of you that feels the need to do this. You will find things to match up with whatever you believe, so before he can hurt you, you can say, "Ah-ha! You cannot fool me. I knew you were an asshole!" Does this sound like a healthy place for your endlessly creative mind to be? Is this a good use of your resources? Absolutely not!

The right relationship brings you peace. There is an underlying current of trust that calms your crazy brain. It is not something that drives you to exhaust yourself with far fetched realities that never come to pass. In the right relationship, you don't have to worry or wonder what he is doing when he is not with you. You trust him to carry himself in a way that honors your relationship. If you cannot trust him, there are two things to consider. Either he is not the right guy, or you are not ready for a healthy relationship and have more inner work to do. Your relationship should be the place you can be calm and centered and relaxed, not the place you go for adrenaline-pumping drama.

If your brain is used to drama, it will find ways to drum it up. This is something you need to address before you enter into healthy relationships. You need to recognize it as a trigger, and if you see yourself slipping back into those old habits of creating stories in your head, you need to fix that in yourself. It is not a man's responsibility to pay the sins of your past relationships. It is not fair to him, and it will exhaust anyone. A good man doesn't put himself in a position to create that kind of hurt in the first place. He doesn't want to see you anxious or make you cry.

If you can remember this, half of the issues you will face will disappear. Truly. I learned this lesson in my forties. Half the stuff you build up in your mind is a monster of your own making. If you approach your guy about it, he will most likely be confused, not having a fucking clue how you went from zero to crazy in your head like that in sixty seconds or less. It amazes me how much dramatic fiction I try to write in my own mind, stories I concoct to explain his cool tone or off-putting behavior when I ask him to do something and he doesn't jump.

Years of drama and pain made my brain very fearful and pushed away at least one really great guy. By getting control over my own head by becoming healthier, I was finally able to attract and maintain a healthy relationship, and you can, too.

The Big Takeaway Question: How much of your time is wasted on creating destructive stories in your head?

If you find yourself doing this, redirect your energy to something else. Shut off your phone for a few hours and do something you enjoy. Go for a walk. Be on the lookout for tendencies to create fictional stories in your head that have no basis in truth.

BAD BOYS ARE BAD FOR A REASON

Who doesn't love a bad boy? This classic cliché gets our motors running almost every time. The dark, tortured, tattooed, motorcycle man, who is alpha as hell—it's a hot stereotype. And I'll be honest; I might have flicked the bean once or twice with one of those in my mind. Just to be clear, there are plenty of amazing tattooed, motorcycle men who are healthy, loving partners. I just used the typical cliché to give you an instant visual.

The real bad boy is one who cannot commit, who is closed off and not emotionally available. It is a man who makes little effort and is using you. The real bad boy breadcrumbs you, giving only tiny morsels of attention, and plays games. He is abusive and angsty and makes your relationship a living hell. He doesn't love himself, so he creates pain in his relationships and drama in his life and drags you into it over and over again.

An interesting exercise is to look at the patterns of the men you are attracted to. Try to approach it from a completely detached place. What attracted you in the first place? What qualities got you obsessed? What drives you into their arms? This will be a very eye-opening exercise. Everyone has a type, to a certain degree, but what if your type is dangerous for you? What if your type makes your mascara run down your face instead of messing up your lipstick? How much self-induced pain are you willing to endure to keep this kind of relationship going?

You might be the type that craves danger, that adrenaline rush of need and want. The physical desire manifested so deeply you can't ignore it because it is burning hot and intense. Like a forest fire ripping through a valley of evergreens, destroying everything in its path, it is all-consuming. A better goal is the slow burn that keeps your heart warm and happy but is safely contained. Opt for a low and slow burn of the coals like when you smoke meat. For hours and hours, you wait, knowing the end result is the most satisfying, succulent, and tender outcome your heart could ever want.

If you find yourself craving the rush, your heart has to relearn how intensity should feel in a normal relationship. It shouldn't be this adrenaline-filled extreme high and low ride with stomach drops, slamming into the curve, and getting whiplash. It's more of a gentle discovery with lower highs and higher lows, but this model is more sustainable. It doesn't burn out your emotions and endocrine system.

I was lucky enough to stumble upon a good guy after my divorce, and he shared the concept of the warm blanket when describing love. He explained that your partner should bring you peace and comfort like a warm blanket fresh from the dryer. This was leagues away from the heart-pounding, adrenaline-fueled love I was used to. If I had heard that in my twenties, I would have yawned. Isn't it funny how twenty years changes everything?

After the pain and chaos of the first forty, I decided that a warm blanket kind of love in my back forty sounded amazing. The partner you choose should give you the most peace and contentment possible. They should be your soft place to fall when the world is harsh and punishing. A place where you can drop your defenses and be accepted while the rest of the world rages in war outside your door. Your love is a fortress. A place you build together, brick by brick, piece by piece until you have created something one of a kind, beautiful, and long-lasting. Anything less would be a disservice.

After decades of chasing bad boys, I developed an appreciation for the nerdy guys. The ones who are smart, but are not dicks about it. Who use their brains instead of their brawn. The guys who systematically approach life as a problem to solve. These thinkers are better husbands, better fathers, and better lovers because they tinker. They test things out. They work at it, day by day, with deliberate effort. This is attractive. This is sustainable. This is the kind of relationship you can build a life around.

The Big Takeaway Question: Are you attracted to bad boys?

Figure out your type. The clues are in your past relationships. Is it time to make a shift?

DON'T BE A CHASER

Men are naturally built to pursue women. That is a drive instilled in them since the beginning of time, when cavemen were driven to chase a woman, beat her with his club, and drag her back to the cave in order to procreate. It is in their DNA. It is who they are, and it is in their nature.

In the early stages of getting to know someone, know that a man who is interested in you will make an effort to see you, be with you, call you, or text you. If he is not doing any of these things, this is not your guy. If you always initiate contact, if you always throw out hints in an attempt to get together, you are wasting your time. If you are unsure about his feelings, step back completely and see what happens. I know, I know, this is the hardest thing in the world to do when you've caught feelings for a guy. When you are constantly checking your texts and refreshing your social media and making sure you haven't accidentally set the phone to silent.

When you do the chasing, it upsets the balance of power. It shakes up the dynamic. Men like a bit of a challenge. When you do all the texting and plan-making, it tells him, "This is an easy one. I don't need to worry about locking down anything with her, so I'll come back to her later." The best thing you can do is ignore the phone and go do something fun that lights you up, because then, if he does call or text, you can talk to him about something exciting. Men love a woman who is doing things and excited and passionate about life. Sitting on the couch, waiting by the phone wastes another precious day in your life. So, go out and do the things, hang out with friends, or do something creative or that you have always wanted to try. Expand your life and make yourself happier, because all that will do is make you healthier and stronger partnership material when the right guy shows up and makes the effort.

Don't interpret a like on Instagram or Facebook as effort. That is the lowest of the low on the scale of effort. That is a man trying to stay relevant and maintaining the tiniest contact, in the case that he finds himself lonely on a Friday night and his number one option is out with her girlfriends. That is how you get exiled to side chick territory, a vast wasteland where women go to die, waiting in full makeup for a late night "Want to hang?" text. You deserve better than that! You deserve a man who makes his intentions known. Who puts in real effort to show you that he wants you in his life. Who isn't always making plans at the very last minute and wanting to chill at your place. You deserve to be the prize he earns with his effort.

Bread-crumbing is as shitty as it sounds. Men that bread-crumb put out tiny little effortless morsels of time and attention, and you gobble them up and yet remain starving, desperate for any little show of attention from him. Ghosting is another crappy modern dating conundrum I hated. When I first started dating again, I caught some feelings for a guy, things began hot and heavy, and then he disappeared for a month on a business trip. When he finally reached out again,

I said, "Hey there, Casper." I can't help it, I'm a smart ass. He found it very offensive, and I laughed my way out of the door and then blocked him. Goodbye Ghost! The truth is that it takes ten seconds to send a text when a man is out of town. If he isn't texting you, then you don't matter. Cut your losses and go find someone who makes you feel like you do.

One of the hardest things to do is to not initiate contact when you like a guy. It is so easy to concoct reasons to contact a guy you like under false pretense, but it doesn't do you any good. If he's your guy, you will sit steady at the top of his mind. He will be dying to reach out to you to hear how your day is going or what you've been doing. If he's not your guy, he won't care, or he will find something more interesting to do. If he wanted to text, he would. If he wanted to call, he would. The most successful and busiest man will always find time for a woman he sees a future with.

Sometimes, you may have to make concessions if he is working on a big project or has something going with his kids. But if days go by and he is not making time to communicate, then he is either not ready, or he is not the right guy. Do not waste your time with either of these guys. Write them off completely, lose their numbers, move on, and open yourself to one that *is* ready and that *is* healthy.

The Big Takeaway Question: Do you initiate all the contact?

Pull back and wait. See what happens. Men are black and white. They are direct and easy to understand. If they want you, nothing will get in their way to have you. If they don't, they will give you excuses. Period.

DON'T GO ALL IN UNTIL HE DOES

In my twenties, I would meet a guy and go on a date, and if my feelings were strongest for him, I would immediately close myself off to all other options and be only available to him. This is the worst idea in the whole wide world. As a result, I had wishy-washy experiences and was frustrated

when I was putting in the effort while they were not. Or waiting on pins and needles to have the "Are you my boyfriend or not?" relationship defining talk.

When I was thrust back out into the dating pool at forty, I decided to play the field on purpose. I went out on a lot of dates with multiple men, then some second or third dates while trying to narrow it down. From the beginning, I was upfront and honest with all the men I dated, and I was not physical with any of them. They all knew I was looking for "the one" and that I wasn't ready to be physical until I was in a monogamous relationship. Some guys didn't like it, and they moved on. That was okay. They were not the guy for me. It was weird at first because part of me felt like I was cheating on the guy who was the number one contestant, but playing the field helped me get to the right guy.

This did a couple of things. Sometimes, it takes a few dates to see if you have a connection with someone. First date jitters sometimes get in the way, and you aren't quite sure. I was brutally honest with myself and with the men I dated. If I knew there was nothing there, I let them know it right away. Those were hard conversations to have, but the men I had them with appreciated the honesty and that I was not wasting anyone's time or money. No one wants to continue to get attached to someone who isn't feeling the same way. Playing the field also gives you the comparison factor. You can test out a few things and see if you line up on certain values before you make a decision.

While I was doing this, I always offered to help pay for whatever dates I was taken on because I think it's the fair thing to do. Some of the guys took me up on it, and some of the guys were old-fashioned and wanted to pay for the whole date. Either way, it gave me some insight into who they were, and it also eliminated the power balance at the end of the night and feeling obligated to do things I wasn't ready to do. Offering to split the check also sends the message to the guy that you are not taking them for granted. You aren't a person who uses people, and you don't expect a man to take care of you. This is the right message to send. No one likes to be used.

When you keep your options open, it motivates the guy to make an actual commitment. He knows you are out there, possibly meeting another man who might prove to be better than him, so if he wants you, he is going to have to get you. The right guy will not be intimidated. He will make that commitment when he is sure, and while you wait, you have more time to make sure he is the right one for you. In the early stages of a relationship, people hide parts of themselves in an effort to present themselves in the best light possible. It's human nature. It takes time to really get to know the real person behind the mask they are showing you. More time to make that decision is never a bad thing. You can collect more evidence to build the case that he is the right guy.

Lopsided love sucks. When you catch feelings that are stronger than what the other person is feeling, it creates an imbalance that makes you feel vulnerable and exposed. By continuing to date other people, you are not so consumed or focused on one person. It gives you an opportunity to take a step back and just enjoy the process. People fall in love at different speeds. Some people run at it with wild abandon, and others take the long way around. Continuing to see other people while you figure this out will give you more data to confirm this is the right relationship for you.

The Big Takeaway Question: Do you go all in before he does?

Play the field with honesty and integrity. Spreading out your attention makes it hard for you to fixate on one and saves you from catching lopsided feelings. When a man wants a woman, he will make a commitment to you. He will not want to continue to share you.

FAST AND FURIOUS

My first several relationships after my divorce were fast and furious, at a breakneck speed that was keeping the adrenaline coursing so much it took my mind off my mess. It was exciting to be swept away in a passionate love that was all-consuming, in a drawing little hearts on my notebooks during conference calls sort of way. But they didn't last. They were destined to crash and burn, and they did.

Chances are really good you have dated one of those passionate types. They are hot, sexy, and fun. There is a spike of all the addictive feel-good chemicals. You know the kind of relationship that starts out on one amazing date, and then he's over every night after that. Within a week, or possibly even a day, he says I love you. Being propelled by the excitement of it all, you say it back because it feels good and the dopamine talked you into it.

The excitement is addictive. It feels good to be wanted and pursued, and all that yummy wanting neediness at first just feels so good, especially if it has been a while since you felt those feelings. It's a rush. The closest feeling to mainlining heroin, I am guessing. And who doesn't want to take a hit of that?

The problem is that things that start this way will likely burn fierce and hot and then burn out and die just as fast. This fast and furious approach to dating is based on chemical reactions and no substance. Getting caught up in all that sexy besotted desire feels good, and that is why we do it. But what if there was a better way?

There is. But you're not going to like it. I didn't, at first, but now I can see why it is so good. Until I met the right guy, I burned hot and fast with nearly every guy I dated. When I met the right guy, he was on such a slow, deliberate path that I was dying. He nearly drove me crazy with his time table. I wanted to be exclusive almost immediately, but he did not. I was ready to say I love you in record time. He was not. I was ready to move in together within six months. He was not.

I was frustrated as hell with him, but a little voice in my head said, "Hmm, we've never done this before. Maybe we should give this a try since your success rate so far is 0%." So, I waited. I calmed my brain that wanted to tell all my friends about my amazing new boyfriend and scream about this relationship from the rooftops. I went out on more dates with other guys to make sure he was the right guy, while he figured out if I was the right girl. This strategy paid off. He is a deliberate decision-maker, and I accepted that about him. He did progress, although ever so slowly, but always forward. It took him a while to hit those milestones, but he never backtracked. When he finally said he loved me, I knew he did and that it meant something to him because it wasn't a phrase he dropped on a whim.

After so many fast and furious relationships, I have finally figured out that this slow burn is perfect and healthy. It has the least amount of drama, and it is solid and secure, built with a strong foundation by a man who knows what he wants and works toward that reality one step at a time.

What are you in such a hurry for anyway? Step off the fast track. At a normal speed, you won't crash and burn. You will be able to make healthy decisions one at a time. You might discover the truth about each other on a realistic timetable that will create a stronger foundation. Or you might discover it's not the right thing without the added financial burden of buying real estate together.

I am finally in a healthy relationship, and I know that it's healthy because it is so different from what I was used to. We took things SLOW in the beginning, and I have to honestly admit it was frustratingly slow, but he was right. He has seen me through some very dark times since we have been together. He is my rock, someone I can always lean on. He is strong and steady and consistent. I was crystal clear with him before we decided to be exclusive. He knows I want to marry again someday, that it is important to me, and even though he has no burning desire to be married, he is working toward that reality with me. We have made progress together, moving in with each other, and someday we have plans to build our dream home. I still get frustrated with time tables. Patience has never been my strong suit, but I have come to appreciate his slow and steady approach. It has led us to a very beautiful place.

The Big Takeaway Question: Are your relationships fast and furious?

Journal about your past relationships and their speed. What was the outcome? Approach the next one more slowly and deliberately.

HE'S NEVER GONNA CHANGE

For years and years, I wanted my ex-husband to change. I begged him to change. I wanted him to stop drinking. I wanted him to stop smoking. He was already sixteen years older than I was, and if he kept it up, who knew how long his body would stay in the game? He was content the way he was, and so this conflicting desire just became an endless source of combat between us that never was resolved. My daughter, who was so wise at the tender age of thirteen, said, "People never change, Mom. They don't."

People can change, but they will only choose to adjust if they want it for themselves. It has to be completely self-driven. It can't come from outside themselves or it will only be temporary. Wanting them to change and constantly spending your energy on convincing them they need to change is a waste.

Entering into relationships with people who have big, glaring qualities that you want to revise is a terrible idea and will only lead to suffering for both of you. Don't be wooed by potential. I hate that word because it becomes a source of angst and frustration. Potential doesn't mean shit. Potential is a might happen, whiff of possibility that can keep you chained to the wrong thing for a long time.

Potential is dangerous because it requires a person to transform to live up to their potential, and that is a recipe for disaster. When you pin your happiness on another person changing, it is putting your happiness in their hands again. It is engaging you in a measuring dynamic, keeping track of if they *are* or are *not* living up to their potential. It is not really your decision if they do or not. No one wants to be with someone who is measuring their output like that. It is draining, and it shifts the dynamic to parent/child or teacher/child, neither of which are good dynamics to have in your relationship.

The only place potential has is in the very early stages, when you are a date or two in and trying to see if you line up. After that, you are hopefully going deeper and not pinning your future on a guy that is okay today, but if he did this, this, and this, he'd be the right one. He may *never* get around to doing any of those things.

Never set yourself up for failure like this. The best thing is to find someone who resonates with you on the big things. Someone who you love "as is" and that you are not dreaming about changing or rescuing. Is there such a thing as a perfect relationship? Of course not, but I finally found the right one, and the reason it is so easy is that we naturally are compatible in almost every aspect, at least with all the biggies. Yet we have enough differences to make it interesting. After years of being in relationships with people that I wanted to fix or change, I can honestly say there is nothing I want to change about this one. This sets you up for success every time.

The only person you can change is yourself. To focus your resources on the idea that, with your love, you can inspire someone else to act differently is a waste of your precious energy. It is hard enough to change things about yourself. The success rate is not that great, but it is infinitely more dismal when you try to change another person. Take responsibility for yourself. Restore and renovate yourself and then find the person who jives with you.

If you are dating, know yourself first and accept that you can't change people. Love them as they are in their default setting or move on to another better fit. The hardest relationship to leave will be the one that is almost the one because you will stay, trying to convince yourself to accept something you want to change about them. Decide early. When the important red flags pop up, exit stage left. Don't talk yourself into staying or, even worse, changing your values to keep the relationship. There is a much better fit out there waiting for you.

The Big Takeaway Question: Do you want to change him?

Think about your relationships in this context. Are you measuring and controlling, thinking things will be perfect if only he changed this one thing?

IF EVERYONE IS A NARCISSIST, YOU'RE NOT READY

Break-ups are painful. Divorce is painful. If you are not healed, you'll drag that cynicism into the next relationship with painful generalizations. All men cheat. All men are narcissistic assholes. The literal odds of that being true are zero percent. It's easy to go completely to the other side of the barometer. On one side is the passive codependent doormat, and on the other is the man-eater with chips on her shoulder a mile high. Extremes are a terrible place to be. Either way, you fall.

When your radar is going off on everything, you aren't open to anything. You are closed off, and any man will find it impossible to scale those walls. If you find yourself here, this is work you need to do to fix yourself and your beliefs before you jump back out into the dating pool. Otherwise, it will just become a frustrating and futile exercise.

I know what you're going to say. "But you said I need to keep my standards high!" Kudos to you for listening. It is true that your standards must be high. But it is also true that you have to open your heart or you will wear out any man, especially the decent ones, who will just fade away because it's too much fucking effort to make anything work with you.

A hostile woman is no fun to date, and nothing meaningful can grow from defensive and suspicious interactions. Your guard does not need to be up constantly, so if it is, you are not ready. You shouldn't be white-knuckling the experience, waiting for the other shoe to drop because it always does. You have to be relaxed and open, with healthy boundaries and standards.

Men are simple. Their thoughts don't circle and spiral out like women's do. They like cause and effect. They like simple and easy. They hate guessing games. They want to make you happy, but sometimes, you need to tell them exactly how to do that. Here is a color-coded map to my g-spot, darling. I joke, but it shocks me how simply they approach life. They don't multi-task. They like to take one project from start to finish. Things with them are always black and white.

Men are people, too. Kinda. Maybe robotic people might be more accurate. Again, I kid, but the truth is that they are looking for a real connection and will step up to make things happen when they find a woman they can't live without. They will jump through some hoops to get you, but don't put out too many hoops or light them all on fire. Work to destroy your own hoops. Work to fix your own issues before you are back out there looking for another lion to tame. Don't label every man an asshole just because of a couple of bad ones. There are good ones out there. Don't chase away the good ones with your impossible standards.

If you think all men are pigs, then you will find pigs. Reset yourself. Deal with your own anger, frustrations, and fears on your own time. Don't drag them into a new relationship. Your slate should be clear. He shouldn't have to make up for anything that isn't his to make up for. You shouldn't smear your worry and distrust onto him because, collectively, that has been your experience with men to date. A healthy man will not stand for that. A healthy man will accept responsibility for what he has done and will work to correct it if he loves you. It is not fair to make him pay for wrongs he never committed in the first place.

The Big Takeaway Question: What are your true thoughts about men and relationships?

Are they negative and suspicious? Then you are not ready. You cannot meet anyone that is a quality human being with those ideas. Clear the slate and start fresh.

FIXER-UPPERS

Take a good hard look at the people you draw into your life. Do you draw in the wounded, the broken, and the weak? It is okay to help. It is good to help. Empaths are the worst at this. As an empath, you want to fix everything, and there is a payoff you get from mending the brokenness, from being the one everyone can count on. It gives your life meaning, fills it with people who need you, and can also become your identity. An identity that doesn't serve you.

You might also find yourself over-helping capable people. Taking the hard work out of their hands and adding it to your pile because you are just so good at it. Just because you are called to help and want to help doesn't mean you should. It will be hard to step back and watch someone struggle, when before they were able to lay their brokenness on your to-do pile. They will cry out and beg, twist reality around, and even accuse you of not loving them. As an empath, you will likely then be guilted into action. This is bad, too.

Relationships are much better when they are level. Like a teeter-totter, the give and take is best when it is even on both sides. That is what you should be striving toward, not being paired up with the kid who jumps off and forces you to go crashing to the ground. You want to pair up with the one who holds space for you gently, who pushes off and lets you soar, and then you do the same for him. It's a steady, mutual give and mutual take. Learn to save your generosity for those who can reciprocate it. For those who bring goodness into your life instead of draining it dry.

A healthy man doesn't need a woman to fix him. He works to fix himself. If you are attracting fixer-uppers into your life, you need to look at your need to be needed. Fixer-uppers should be avoided because they are endlessly frustrating to renovate. You will slave away and try to control and fix, and at the end of it all will likely just end up with a man who resents you. An unhealthy partner will lean too much on the other person, and this creates a shift that will kill the relationship. It fosters bitterness, anger, and resentment. It shifts the relationship to a child/parent place that is deadly for your sex life.

Fixer-uppers keep you busy. So busy. Busyness can be a trauma response because, if you stay busy enough, you don't have the time, energy, or resources to focus on yourself. You will lack the cool, clear thinking to notice what you are doing isn't healthy. One of my therapists said to me once, "What if you took all that energy that you use trying to fix everyone else's stuff and focused those resources on yourself for a while?" I laughed, because I laugh when I am nervous, and the thought of all that selfishness focused on me made me uncomfortable. I am the type of girl who's wearing yoga pants from eight years ago and who drove the junkiest minivan for years because I didn't think any of my resources were supposed to be used to make my life better. I am getting better at this. It is so much easier to identify when I slip, and I do slip. It is a battle to see with fresh eyes what is actually happening and what part I am playing in it. It is so easy to slip into the familiar, even if you know on every level the familiar is unhealthy. The difference is by being able to identify unhealthy behaviors now, you can finally readjust and realign with the new principles you want in your life.

It is good to give. But learn to give in a healthy way and pick the right people to save. That will make all the difference.

The Big Takeaway Question: Are you drawn to fixer-uppers?

Why? It's hard to admit this. Refocus that fixing desire to fix things in your own life.

CARE TAKE OVERS

Are you a caretaker? The kind of person who loves to help, who is always looking for ways to lighten other people's loads? Do you put others' needs ahead of your own? Do you give and give and give until it hurts?

It's great to give. It feels so good to give and be generous, but the unfortunate fact of life is that givers usually get paired up with takers. Everything is nice and sunny when you meet, the oxytocin is flying, and the giver gives as she is naturally made to do while the taker takes as he is naturally made to do, and everything is perfect until the giver's bucket is empty. The giver will scrape every last drop of herself out and pour it on the taker, and the taker will allow it because that is what takers do.

Just like I encourage you to work on yourself so you can present the best, healthiest, smartest parts of yourself, the man you are with should be doing the same. Unhealthy partners can be users who are looking for care-taking because they do not want to grow up and handle it themselves. I used to think care-taking was a noble quality in a person, but now as a middle-aged woman, I can absolutely tell you it is the fast track to Pain Town. I lived to take care of the people in my life. I was so good at anticipating needs and jumping up to fill them like it was my duty. Over time, I got frustrated and resentful about it, yet still continued to do this because it was a pattern of behavior that was so ingrained in me, it was second nature.

I have had to take a long hard look at myself and how my penchant for care take overs is impacting my life and those that are closest to me. I had to evaluate what it was doing to my romantic relationships, what it was doing with my kids. It spilled out onto every aspect of my life and was the reason I was so exhausted. Taking care of other people is fucking exhausting. So why did I do it? Because I got a pay-off. It made me feel more valuable as a person. It made me feel more selfless. I felt like I was doing the right thing, when nothing could be further from the truth. It took almost two decades to see this was a destructive pattern of behavior, not just for me, but for the people I poured all that care-taking on. It allowed them to skate through life, to avoid all the pesky responsibilities and soul-sucking minutia that life entails. I can't believe it took me so long to see that.

Care take overs aren't caring at all. Instead, they are weakening for everyone. They tie the other person to you in a sick way forever, or for as long as you are willing to participate. When you help people do things that they are completely capable of doing on their own, it makes them doubt their own abilities. Everyone suffers in this dynamic.

When I finally started dating a healthy guy, he didn't need my help at all. He was successful at going through life without me already, and it was the most foreign thing in the world to me. It felt awkward as hell. "What do you mean you don't need me to set up your dental exam and drive you there?" The awkwardness was a bright spotlight on how unhealthy things had been, and I struggled to adjust at first. I was used to anticipating needs and filling them without being asked. When I met a guy who didn't need me to take care of him, it was eye-opening for me. What in the hell? You can wash the dishes and know how to file your taxes? You know how to check your credit report and how online bill pay works?

I was literally taken aback. The doing I was normally consumed by in my other relationships suddenly was unnecessary. It left me a little lost. Who am I now that I have another capable adult in my life who doesn't need me to do things for him? What am I supposed to do with myself now that I don't have the to-do list of two people? I refocused that energy on myself and on my kids. I sat in the quiet of less responsibility, grappling with my need to be needed.

I still love to do things for the people I love, but now it comes from a healthy place. Instead of over-giving and doing things for my teenagers out of guilt from my divorce, I am a resource. I force them to fill out their own forms and make their own appointments. I cook one meal a day. After that, they can make their own. I still love doing things for my guy, but the awesome thing is he loves doing things for me, too. Since I have lived without a partner who reciprocates for so long, it is something I will never take for granted. I appreciate every little thing he does for me. This is healthy. This feels so good.

The Big Takeaway Question: Are you participating in care take overs?

Take a breath and a step back. Don't rush in to help every time. Instead of anticipating the needs of others, give them time to figure it out.

WHAT RED FLAGS?

I was standing in a field of red flags, relationship after relationship, yet unable to see a single one. Naive or just plain stupid? Honestly, either of those terms applied. There was the guy that, two weeks into the relationship, during a post-coitus confession, admitted to being the leader of an extremist fringe group on the internet. According to him, it was a non-issue because it had dissolved and wasn't part of his life anymore. A healthy person would have run away from that, screaming, "Lose my number," out the window as she squealed out of the parking lot, burning rubber. Not me. I hung in there for a year and a half. A year and a half! (Insert eye roll here because I deserve it.)

There was the guy who I accidentally discovered was monitoring my internet use, websites I went to, and digging through my digital footprint without my permission, just to make sure I wasn't cheating on him. I wasn't.

There was the guy who had an 'incident' on his record, after being caught up in a prostitution sting. My response was, "Everyone makes mistakes."

I could go on and on. I truly made a lot of mistakes with

men. Relationships are tricky to navigate because, in the early stages, there is so much deceit. And it's not always intentional. It is just a product of putting your best foot out there, painting yourself in a better light to sell the merchandise. Eventually, over time, you can't keep up the appearances, and you start to show your partner who you really are in your words and actions. Sometimes, you are so stuck with the gooey-eyed love goggles on that the other person could admit to killing a man and you would counter with, "He's changed now. That was in the past. He's not the same guy." I am exaggerating a bit to prove my point, but it is amazing what people will let slide in their desire to couple up.

Red flags are closely linked to your intuition. You know that feeling of the hairs on the back of your neck prickling up, or that feeling in your tummy that says, *hmm, something is not right here*? That is your intuition, raising a red flag and telling you to run the fuck away. The problem is that most train wrecks have stopped listening to their intuition long ago. You've tuned it out or turned it down so low that you can't even hear your inner voice anymore. The red flags have become invisible through your rose-colored glasses. The thing is that your intuition is usually never wrong. It's that centuries honed fight or flight mechanism that has helped your ancestors survive as mankind progressed through new eras of human development. The problem is that modern-day man is so distracted from it with all the things vying for our attention. Recognizing the red flags and then being brave enough to course correct when you see danger early on is the key.

Red flags pop up to warn you about danger, but if you doubt yourself, you often ignore them. Then years can pass, and you wonder, *How the hell did I get here?* It's easy to coast through life, to put the blinders on and self-soothe with your favorite diversion. These activities distract you from the red flags, put you in a time warp and fully into victim mode. You don't think things can change, or you don't want to face the hard work it takes to make real changes, and so you numb out and try to forget.

If you can't see them, your friends can. With their level of detachment from the gooey-eyed lovey-dovey-ness of a new relationship, they can see these issues more clearly. If your friends have a problem or tell you there is a red flag, you need to really pay attention. If there are things you avoid telling your friends about the person you are dating because you know they will be in your face about it, that is a red flag. If you are afraid to ask your friends what they truly think of the person you are dating, that is a red flag. The people who love you want the best for you. A good friend will tell you when you are fucking up, hopefully over many, many medicinal margaritas. Sometimes, your friends are afraid to tell you the truth. My best friends and my sister all avoided telling me they had concerns about my ex-husband. I wish I had asked them, and I wish I had been open enough to listen to what they said, knowing that they were saying those things because they love me. It would have saved me nearly two decades.

When you don't love yourself enough or trust yourself enough you can see the red flags, you can feel the goosebumps, yet you will do something counterintuitive. You will allow people to stay that aren't good for you, reduce your standards, break your deal breakers, and wear yourself down.

Make it easy on yourself and see the red flags. They don't go away. The red flags you first saw when you began dating are the reasons you break up, but sometimes you can waste fifteen years ignoring them. Red flags that accumulate breed chaos in your life. A crucial equation to commit to memory is IGNORING RED FLAGS = CHAOS. Do you want peace?

Value yourself enough to see red flags and take appropriate action. Stop giving too many chances to people who disrespect your boundaries, who take more than they give. Don't allow your standards to erode.

Everyone has a standard, even if they think they don't. It is what you allow, whether your standards are high or low or in-between. Every relationship and human that you have interacted with knows consciously or subconsciously what your standards are. Every day, they communicate that to you in the words they use and the way they treat you.

Standards are the minimum, the bare minimum that you require, and most people will only perform to the standard. So, what is your standard? In my twenties, they were pretty low. As a result, my relationships were weak and underwhelming, leaving me scrambling and settling. The men who showed up cheated on me, lied to me, and used me because I allowed them to. I couldn't blame them because I set up a system that allowed it to happen.

Standards and red flags have a very symbiotic relationship. With high standards, there will be few to no red flags, while with low standards, there will be more red flags. As with everything, I will encourage you to set your bar in a healthy place. Not impossibly high that no man could clear it, but leave room for error. He is human and will make mistakes. Being at the extreme end of either spectrum is not a healthy place to be.

When you build your life with someone who's covered in red flags, it's like building your dream home on quicksand. You will spin out, putting crazy effort into making the home beautiful for everyone to see, but the foundation is flawed. It will never support the home you are struggling to create. One day, a storm will come and wash it out to sea.

Open your eyes to the red flags early. Don't make excuses for them. Use them as they are intended, a warning to stop.

Making decisions faster will become easier with time. Acknowledging the red flags and taking swift action will open you back up to finding a more suitable partner.

The Big Takeaway Question: Can you identify red flags early?

Be honest. Admit if there are times you avoided them or didn't see them and what the outcome was. Tap into your inner wisdom, and when you see one, value yourself enough to take action immediately.

YOUR (GIRL)FRIENDS KNOW

They do and they also want what is best for you. That combo may make their advice incredibly hard and painful to hear when you're head over heels in love with the man you think is Mr. Right, but who your girls know without a doubt is Mr. Wrong.

Think about your closest friends. These are the chosen few you've decided to do life with. They will celebrate your ups and commiserate with you during the downs. There is no motive there except for their love and unwavering support of you. They are on your side. Forever and for always. They are on the lookout for red flags, the ones you ignore when he flashes you the dimples. They can see things that you refuse to acknowledge or can't see in your current besotted state. You see what you want to see when you are in love. They aren't all love drunk and invested in anything that doesn't bring you happiness. They don't give a rip who this guy is you've brought into the crazy. They are only interested in how he treats you and what you are like around him. They want to see you be yourself around him, and to be loved for it. You can't fool your friends because they know the authentic you. They know your history and where the bodies are buried.

The right guy will bring out the best in you. He will encourage your hopes and dreams, however wild and crazy they may be. He will be a shoulder to lean on when things get heavy and life is coming for you. The right guy makes a woman glow from the inside out. She will radiate because that is what women do when they are loved properly. Your friends want you to discover this kind of love because they know it is best for you.

Sometimes, the people closest to you are afraid to speak up about the things they see because they are afraid of losing the friendship, or they are afraid of the way you will react. Before making any kind of long-term commitment, it definitely helps to have a frank conversation with your closest friends and get their honest opinions, but the catch is that you need to be in a frame of mind to receive what they say without feeling attacked. You need to be open and come to the conversation knowing these people love you. There is no ulterior motive in whatever they say. You need to go into this conversation without excuses and with your ears and heart wide open. Your best friends will tell you the truth as they see it, and their detached perspective is helpful.

If they have concerns, don't offer excuses and explain them away. Don't try to manipulate the way they think of your guy by the information you share or don't share. Listen and then later, when you can come back to their opinions in a completely unemotional state, walk through their concerns. Likely, your friends have known you for years, maybe even decades. They know what kind of guy you need, and if you ask them, they will be happy to tell you.

If you find yourself twisting the truth, or leaving important information out when you talk to your friends, he is not the right guy. Like a drug addict wanting the next hit, you can manipulate the truth and twist the situation to be acceptable in your mind. You can find yourself coming back for hit after hit of something that is all wrong for you and be unable to stop yourself. It's amazing, your mind's ability to see the truth as you want to see it, or to paint the picture or write the story you want to tell.

If your love drunk reality is like a funhouse mirror, all distorted and twisted up, your friends are the mirror in the changing room that shows every varicose vein and stretch mark. The people closest to you can provide a reality check for you. They have no skin in the game, so their unbiased opinions matter. If they tell you he's bad for you, save yourself the heartache and the possible decades of pain and listen.

Your friends know.

The Big Takeaway Question: What do your friends think?

Don't ever discount what someone who truly loves you has to say about the guy you are dating. They are almost never wrong.

BUT WE'VE BEEN TOGETHER FOR YEARS... THE LIE OF TIME

It's hard to walk away from a commitment, especially if you have sunk years of your life into it. The tough reality is that, if you've already wasted twenty years in the wrong job or the wrong relationship and you decide to stick it out, you will likely waste another twenty.

You can get to the deeply settling place of acceptance. Acceptance of a standard that is unacceptable, because changing course and going a different way is hard, especially in midlife and when it affects other people. So many people stay in things that don't make them happy or don't serve who they are anymore. You may find yourself stuck right now, paralyzed for years by fear of making another bad choice. Starting completely over becomes terrifying, but that is exactly why you should.

It's easy to settle. Most people do. I did. You might have. But as a former settler, I can say that the life that I am currently living fills me with so much joy, happiness, and gratitude and was worth every painful consequence I went through. (And if you read my memoir, you know there were many). I knew things were bad for years, and yet I wasted so much time because I accepted and settled.

In the settle state, you go numb to what is happening and you cut yourself off from experiencing the fullness and joy of life. It is easy for years to pass because you will reach for things to make the settling more palatable. These things will distract you into feeling happy enough, good enough, settled enough.

That is a terrible place to be because real change only happens when you get uncomfortable. The life softeners you choose don't allow you to get to that place of pain where you say, "Not one more fucking day! I deserve better than this!" If you are happy enough, you will never get there. The place of pain can lead you to your greatest happiness. It can be the kick in the ass you need to massively remodel your life. To make the changes and cut the people out who have been phoning it in.

Time can lull you to complacency. It can tell you that this is good enough. It can bring fear to a fevered pitch when you consider having to start all over. Starting over from square one is a terrifying prospect when you think half your life is already over. Beginning again, so long in the tooth, can be so scary that the easier decision is to just settle in and let the rest of your years lull you back to sleep like a baby in a car seat on the highway.

I can tell you that if you are brave enough to radically love yourself enough to completely gut what isn't working in your life and then focus on your own health and healing, you will live a life filled with such joy and peace and clarity it will blow your mind. It is there for the taking if you can roust yourself enough to wake up and do the things that you've been putting off for years and years.

Time is a commodity. It doesn't spool out forever. You have a finite amount of it. Like it or not, you are walking through your life right now with an invisible expiration date on your forehead. A clock that is ticking down to the end. You don't get to take a time-out. It endlessly ticks closer to your final destination. That should scare the hell out of you. If you are a fence sitter or are sitting in a cesspool of indecision, that should coerce you into motion. How much of your life do you want to waste? Every day, you get up and make that decision whether you think you make it or not.

You deserve more. Don't settle. Don't waste a single moment more inside the things that don't fit you. Shed the old and welcome the new. Step into the bigger, brighter, bolder you that has been waiting for the chance to shine. Don't buy into the lies.

The Big Takeaway Question: Where have you settled? Are you letting fear of the do-over get in your way?

List the times you have settled for less than you deserve in your life. It is scary to start over, especially after forty when you likely have other little people depending on you. Feel the fear and do it anyway because the time is going to pass whether you like it or not. The best time to start something new was yesterday. The second-best time is today.

KNOW WHEN TO FOLD 'EM

How much of your life do you want to waste? A day, a year, a decade? It's possible to find yourself in a place where you are wasting multiple decades, paralyzed by indecision. Unable to make a change because you are afraid of the unknown. Sometimes, you will suffer decades in the known, afraid to break free and find the person that energizes you, lifts you up, and is a partner in every sense of the word. You fear that finding a person like that is like finding a unicorn, completely unattainable, unrealistic, and so you stay stuck. Indecision is also a decision. Staying in something because you are afraid to start over or are terrified of being alone brings misery to your doorstep.

One of my best friends, Amy, is the healthiest person I know. When she started dating again, she told me she was ruthless. If she didn't connect or she saw a potential problem, she cut him loose and moved right on to the next one. I was a pleaser, so when I started dating after my divorce, I gave men too many chances. I dated guys for longer than I should have in an effort to be sweet and nice.

Before I met the right guy, I found myself single again

after I had taken a solid six months to be alone, and I decided to try a little experiment. I adopted Amy's approach. If we went on a first date and there was no chemistry, I cut him loose. It was the first time in my life I didn't settle. After one date with a really nice guy, who checked a lot of my boxes but the chemistry wasn't there, he walked me to my car and asked to see me again. Instead of accepting another date and suffering through something I knew was going to be like dating my brother, I told him the truth. I said, "You're great and I had an awesome time meeting you, but I just don't think we have what I am looking for." He shocked me by thanking me for not wasting his time or his money on another date that would go nowhere.

Good men like the truth, girls. They would much rather you be upfront and honest instead of stringing them along. They get their hopes up, too, and most of the time, our wants are insanely more specific and lengthier than a man's. They want someone who is drama free to have fun with that they find attractive, and that's about it. Just to be clear, attractive to most men has a very different meaning than what the media and photoshopped magazines try to sell to you.

After that awkward lesson, it got easier to make those ruthless decisions, to cut them loose right away when I knew it wasn't right. Every decision I made, made it easier to make more decisions. It's like training a muscle. With practice, it gets stronger.

Rejection is your friend. It is decisive, freeing you to move on to something that is more aligned with you. Whether you are rejected or you do the rejecting, it truly is a gift. It doesn't leave room to wonder and waffle. Rejection brings closure and allows you to move on to something more compatible. Don't wallow in the sorrow of rejection. Invite it in and thank it for showing up so quickly. It gave you the gift of complete redirection and saved you precious time.

If you struggle with ending the wrong things, you likely don't trust yourself. You are holding on to old beliefs and backing them up with the evidence of times you didn't make the right decision. Let that go. Be bold, trust your gut and end it, and then let it go. Don't revisit it and rub the regret all over your heart. Embrace what is next fully. You never know what will come around the next corner.

The Big Takeaway Question: Do you stay in the wrong relationships longer than you should?

If you do, you must examine your standards. Why do you stay in relationships that don't fit you? How much of your life are you willing to waste?

CLEAN BREAKS

There aren't many clean breaks anymore. Social media, hook-up culture, and texting make it nearly impossible to end the wrong relationship completely. There are side chicks, friends with benefits, and endless ways to stay kind of engaged with someone that is totally wrong for you. It's so easy to fall back into what you know. The average but semi-satisfying sex instead of not knowing when you'll get some again. The slippery slope of maintaining contact and being "friends." NO! NO! NO! You have enough friends. The only reason to stay friends with an ex is to have someone to bang when options are few or you want to have a plan B.

My therapist talked about the concept of invisible strings connecting us to everyone in our lives. These invisible threads bind you tightly to each other, and even when the dynamics are sick, you struggle to cut yourself free. The very best possible thing you can do after a break-up is to delete the ex from everything. Block him if you have to. Erase them from your phone. Get out the giant scissors that they have on hand for ribbon-cutting ceremonies and cut yourself completely free.

People like to keep doors open. Mom will tell you, "Don't burn any bridges." But what if those bridges should be burnt down to stop the sad and lonely from running back across them in the dark when the night is long and there is no one to hold you? When the twilight hours are so sad and lonely that any warm body is better than none? There is a reason you break up with a person. If the relationship has enough problems that you can't tolerate it anymore and break up, that should be the end. You should move on. But many times, you don't because your brain plays a trick on you and decides to only show you the highlights reel with the sweet romantic montage when you are sad and lonely. Not the hidden camera footage of him picking his nose, searching through your phone without permission, and kicking your dog. Your brain will play tricks on you, and as long as the bridge is there, it will give you reasons to run across it.

Burn that motherfucker down. Today. Make it impossible to go back. That is the only way. Don't be friends, don't help them move, and don't offer to dog sit. Restrict access completely. Don't like their photo on Instagram, and don't obsess over their latest gym selfie. Burn that motherfucker down.

Clean breaks allow for healing. You know when a tree is struck by lightning, and it has a messy scar, and half of it is growing and trying to survive, and half of it is dead? The best thing for it and for you is to cut away the old, down to the first healthy branch, and allow the healing to begin.

Without a clean break, it also makes it impossible to attract the right guy because there is an energy of messiness that you will project. You won't be able to attract a good one because your energy is divided. Stuck between two worlds, you have one foot in the bed of the old guy while the rest of you searches for the right one. A girl has needs. I totally get that, but get yourself a toy and cut every tie to the wrong one to free up your energy to attract the right one.

You don't have to be friends with an ex. Ever. In fact, if you are considering it, I would recommend a hiatus for at least a year. Then you can re-evaluate with fresh eyes whether they are truly a friend or if they are a crutch that you are leaning on to get through those lonely nights. Don't be wishy-washy. Be decisive and cut those people out of your life with surgical precision. Clean breaks are the fastest way to finding a healthy relationship. Quit sabotaging yourself by staying involved or connected to the past. Cut yourself free and step into a brand new future, free from the strings that will try to hold you back. Live your life unencumbered by the messy web of loose ties to the past. It doesn't serve you.

The Big Takeaway Question: Have you made a clean break with your past relationships?

If you haven't, why not? Of course, if you have kids together, this is harder. But the same rules apply. Don't invite them back into your bed or hold space for them in your heart.

HEALTHY NEEDS

In a healthy relationship, there are healthy needs of each partner. Any relationship works because of the willingness of the partners to provide these needs.

Safety, security, respect, an identity of your own, communication, honesty, and truth. Playfulness, equality, comfort, empathy, trust, and compassion. These are all examples of healthy needs. If your relationship is lacking in these areas, fix them or move on. I mean that.

Any relationship is two people entering into an agreement to provide or enhance these things for the other. The hard part is there are two different people with two totally different requirements deciding to do life together. Because of the differences, conflicts will naturally arise. Sometimes your needs will take a backseat to your partner's, and vice versa. It's a give and take and a willingness to step up and provide these things that makes a relationship work. If you tell someone directly what your needs are and they do not make an honest attempt to fill those, then they are not your person. Love is giving someone what they need in a healthy way. It is showing up and protecting someone else's heart. It is making an effort and an agreement to hold their heart in your hands.

When relationships pass the test of time, you will see all of these things woven together over years and years. Where you have spent so much time growing and learning about each other and life, together. Sometimes, you will take the reins and do most of the work, and other times, your partner will. That is natural and normal as you grow together. It is truly beautiful the tapestry you can make from this shared place, weaving in beautiful colors as you go. It takes time to create something unique and substantial, and it takes a willingness to show up every day and make the effort.

Not all days will be easy. Life teaches you many lessons. Sometimes, your world will be rocked to the core and you will rely more on your partner, and sometimes, it will happen to them. Occasionally, it will happen to you both at the same time. The key is to turn toward each other in these key moments instead of away. If you pull away or individualize yourself too much, then the relationship will suffer. Over time, if you distance yourself too much, it becomes harder to sync back up and grow with each other.

As you go through life, it is natural to change and grow and to become someone different as the decades march on. The key is to grow together and to grow toward each other instead of away. If you grow away, you may find yourself alone years later, wondering why you continue to stay when you feel so lonely. Sometimes people grow up and don't fit together anymore. Usually, this is for one of two reasons. Either they were not honest with themselves or didn't know themselves enough when they entered into the relationship, or they turned away from their partner for so long that to turn back was impossible.

In Gilroy, California, there is a place where a man named Axel Erlandson has grafted trees together to form basket shapes and other interesting forms. These trees are truly works of art. The term is called inoculation and occurs when one tree bonds to another. This man purposefully grafted the trees together to create whimsical shapes. It was a lengthy process, taking years and years of pruning, shaping, and grafting, but over decades, they have become so beautiful that people come from far and wide to see them.

It is a very similar process in a healthy relationship. It takes years and years of pruning and grafting as you choose to grow together instead of apart. You have your own healthy roots, and your partner has his, but combined together, they can become something magnificent. Something that is more beautiful as a whole than the individual parts. It's not easy. It takes work. It takes time and resilience. It takes dedication, but after decades of growing together, you will have created something beautiful that people come from miles to see.

The Big Takeaway Question: What are your needs?

Inventory all of your needs. What do you need to be happy and feel safe and secure? Don't judge them, just write them down. Then figure out your why. Why do you need each of these needs? Then rewrite the list in order of importance for you. Label each need as flexible or inflexible, healthy or damaging.

This will give you a concrete list to work from as well as illuminate the internal work you need to do to heal the unhealthy needs. As you meet potential partners, you can use this list to gauge compatibility and to spell out clearly what you need from a partner when you have progressed enough to have a serious conversation about the future.

PARTNERSHIPS

If you try to set up a business, experts will tell you that the partnership is the most difficult type of business classification to make successful. I think this is also true in life. Partnerships are difficult because they depend on two entities or people showing up and doing what is required to keep the business intact and functioning. So many businesses dissolve partnerships because one party or the other feels slighted, and then feelings get in the way and the business is doomed.

Partnerships are hard, especially if you are the type of person who hated group projects in school. I know I did, mostly because I always got stuck with a slacker who would refuse to pull their weight and so I ended up doing the work of two people with half the credit. The same is true in relationships. If you don't want to be stuck doing the work of two people, you need to choose your partner carefully. Look at all the factors—finances, sex, religion, etc.... Weigh these values in the order of importance for you. There are no wrong answers. It requires truth and honesty of where your own heart lies.

The easiest partnership will be with someone whose values align with yours. Someone who sees the world the same way you do. Someone on the same team, pulling toward the same goal. I have been in so many relationships that were skewed in this area, where I did not line up with my partner, and let me tell you it is painful. The amount of effort it takes in comparison with a partner that you line up with is leagues apart. Life is challenging enough on its own. Every partnership is tested in different ways, and it is so much easier to face challenges together and with a united front. Choosing the best partner will give you someone to turn to when the wind whips and the hurricanes beat at your door. Someone who will protect and comfort you when deep in the pit of fear themselves.

Partnerships survive because both parties pull their own weight. They bring effort and intention to the relationship. They work hard in ways that complement their partner in a symbiotic dance. Partnerships that die are lopsided, where one person is in it, working toward the goal themselves, but the other one is MIA or distracted. It takes real concentrated daily effort to make a partnership survive. It is the constant focus and eye on the mission statement that keeps the partnership on the right track.

Partnerships survive based on communication, trust, and hard work. Partnerships that fail die based on selfishness, laziness, and neglect. Choose your partner wisely and then pull your own weight.

The Big Takeaway Question: Are you partnership material?

There definitely is an ebb and flow in any relationship, but partnerships thrive when both parties strive to bring their best to the table at least most of the time. Look at your current relationship or ones in your past and evaluate them for healthy partnership status. What did you do right? What do you need to work on to be a more solid partner?

HOLD MY HAND WHILE I FIX MYSELF

I failed at many relationships after my divorce. After being off the market for twenty years, it was strange being back in the dating pool with other broken people, trying hard to sift for the gold but mostly finding fools—myself included since I was probably the biggest fool of all. People told me to take some time for myself and to heal myself, and I was like, "No way, I have been in a bad place for years. I am ready to feel good again," and so I chased that and I dated.

Downloading apps, texting, and occasionally sexting (hey, I have a naughty streak and can't help myself). It was a high to get external validation from men. Who doesn't love to be wooed? It felt great. After years of feeling numb, it was fun, and I became so good at flirty texting that it was an enjoyable pastime for me. I rushed into relationship after relationship, each one crashing and burning. The reason they crashed and burned was because I expected the other person to fix my emotional state.

For a long time, I put my happiness in the hands of the man I was dating. My mood was determined by his actions, good or bad. Finally, I figured out that putting this power in the hands of my lover was a terrible way to live, not to mention too much pressure and stress on him. He's not qualified to do that, yet I was making it his responsibility. When I pulled that responsibility off his plate and added it back to mine, there was a complete shift in the happiness factor of the relationship.

Now, I just want him to hold my hand while I fix myself. When things go wrong in life, I don't need him to fix anything. I just need his quiet strength and support. When I first started dating my forever guy, and problems arose, he tried to fix things for me. He is very solutions-oriented, a natural troubleshooter in his career, and early on when things were difficult with the kids or my ex or work, he would spin out solution after solution thinking that was what I needed. Through communication, I was able to tell him that was *not* what I needed. I just wanted comfort. I wanted a hug and a shoulder to cry on when things got too hard. I wanted him to say, "You are strong, and you can do this," when I was struggling to fix it on my own. He understands this now and gives me what I need in those moments. He knows I don't need solutions from him unless I directly ask for one.

Expecting someone to fix your problems is the fast track to failure in your relationships. It is not their job. You shouldn't be a fixer-upper looking for an investor, and neither should he. You should continually strive to fix yourself, garnering support from your partner. Fixing takes energy, and if it's a major soul-remodeling project, you might need to take yourself off the market to do it. That is time well spent because, when you re-list yourself, you will find much better offers flying in from healthier humans.

Fixing yourself begins with an inventory of what repairs need to be done, then methodically committing the time to yourself to carry them out. Focus on one project at a time so you can finish it completely. Sometimes, you won't see the damage until you are inside a relationship. Being with another person will often bring things forward that have been hidden. If you are inside a healthy relationship, you *can* do the work. It is harder, but it can be done. It starts with an honest conversation, telling him exactly what you need and what you are trying to do. The more truthful and vulnerable you can be, the better.

Healthy men are simple. They like the truth. They want to know what the real problem is and will do their best to support you fixing it on your own. Healthy men like directness and solution-driven information. You might need to spell it out. I am working through _____, and I need _____ from you. I know that sounds simple, but it is true. Simplicity is good, for everything. Don't dance around it, and don't send him a message to decode. State what you are trying to fix and what you need in as few words as possible, and he will work to provide that. Healthy men want to see you happy and will be so relieved that they are not fully responsible for it.

The Big Takeaway Question: Are you putting your happiness in the hands of someone else?

Why are you doing that? Don't give that kind of power to someone else. Take back that responsibility and be the master of your own happiness. Fix yourself.

ARE YOU A FLOWER OR A GARDENER?

I love to garden. Being in the sun, digging in the dirt is my happy place. Creating something beautiful out of the earth and hard work is so rewarding for me. I was not surprised to see this translate into my relationships.

If you have a relationship between a flower and a gardener, this will be successful for a time. The gardener will enjoy taking care of the flower, giving the flower everything it needs to thrive—water, sun, and fertilizer. The flower will flourish with all this attention and become more beautiful, growing taller and faster and more vibrant, until the gardener tires.

If you have a relationship between a flower and a flower, it is doomed from the beginning. All the weeds will grow around you. You will be self-focused, out for yourself, hoarding whatever water you can, saving all the fertilizer around you so you can grow as big as possible, but the weeds will eventually take over. The neglect will destroy you both, crowding you out with thorny thistles that grow twice as fast as you do. The fast-growing weeds will overshadow you and suck all of the sun out of your life. Sometimes, one flower will grow bigger and showier than the other, and the less-nourished flower will wither and die on the vine.

If you have a relationship between a gardener and another gardener, then this is perfection. No one person has to shoulder all the work. You can split up the tasks and grow together. Your effort is multiplied, giving you each the ability to flourish. You can each settle into the sun when you need to rest and reap the joy of being cared for. It is a beautiful way to live.

A flower is beautiful because it is cared for by the gardener. You were born a flower, unable to thrive and take care of yourself. As you grow, if you are healthy, you develop emotional maturity that teaches you to value the practice of gardening. That instant gratification doesn't always work. That you must reap and then sow. It teaches you patience and that there is a season for everything. There is a spring to plant and a fall to harvest for a reason. All of these lessons will make you a better gardener.

Don't get distracted by a showy flower, one that is consumed by beauty and the materialistic displays of it. That is why the beautiful in our society get a pass. They are not expected to develop the other sides of their personalities, which often leaves them gorgeous but stunted. When their flower starts to fade, they are terrified because then the deeper parts of themselves are on display and they now are not as breathtakingly beautiful as their beautiful blooms once were. They bloomed early, and now, in the fall of their lives, they find themselves unfulfilled and frustrated and having to relearn how to be in society or perish.

Everyone loves a beautiful orchid in full bloom, but not everyone is willing to do the work months in advance to enable the orchid to bloom in the first place. There's day to day tending to what looks like a dead stick in order to give it what it needs to be breathtakingly beautiful again. Cultivating your gardening abilities is something you will hone over your lifetime. Yes, the flower is beautiful, but even more so is the dedication and care that the gardener provides in order for it to bloom.

Find yourself a fellow gardener and focus on developing these qualities in yourself. A gardener is patient and kind. A gardener is hopeful and earnest. A gardener is optimistic and dedicated, someone who can sit in the great gray deadness of winter and see the future garden bursting with hope and a cacophony of color. Who knows the trees will bud again, and the lime green leaves will surface when the sun eventually comes back out. A gardener is the best person to survive a desolate winter with, someone who covers up the roses and brings the house plants back inside, who is secure in the knowledge that if they take care of them they will bloom again.

The Big Takeaway Question: Which are you in your relationships, the flower or the gardener? How can you develop more gardening habits?

It's helpful to look at your patterns in your previous relationships. Did you find yourself toiling away, doing all the hard stuff alone? Did you need constant care, or were you called spoiled? Identify the men you have had relationships with. Were they gardeners or flowers?

ZODIAC SIGNS, LOVE LANGUAGES, AND MYERS BRIGGS PERSONALITY TEST

I turned to science when it was time to date after my divorce. I'll be the first to admit that the zodiac isn't an exact science, but as I have studied my own sign, Cancer, I have found that it has nailed me. It is spot on, exposing my weaknesses and my strengths the majority of the time. So, I actually decided to use that tool as a guide to decide who to date. Cancer is most compatible with Pisces, Scorpio, and Taurus. I literally put it in my dating profile that I was only interested in dating these three signs. This fact was met with interesting perspectives. A few people called me crazy. A few people were excited if they were in the chosen few. It was one barometer to see how they reacted to my criteria.

When I was actively dating, I always asked about love languages. My top two are physical touch and acts of service. The guy I am with now is exactly the same. Is that a requirement? No. But it is so much easier to give love the same way that you like to receive it. It is not second nature for me to shower someone with praise or compliments, and gift-giving is an anxiety-producing game of torture. I'm an introvert, so quality time is me, by myself, preferably in a hammock by the ocean with a huge stack of books on my kindle app and a margarita. But I love a hug and will do nearly anything for the person who saves me time by backing up my computer without being asked. If you don't line up with your partner, it's okay. It will just take more work and concentrated effort. It won't come naturally, and you will have to think about it more.

I also love the Myers Briggs Personality test. After taking the online test, you can learn a wealth of information about yourself as well as anyone who tells you their type. I am an INFJ. It nails me, too, and when my guy told me his type, it also gave me so much insight into who he is and what makes him tick. I find this kind of thing endlessly fascinating.

Do any of these things ensure success? No. Nothing does. What it did do was give me tools to make a choice that was naturally compatible from the get-go. I wanted things to be easier the next time around. I didn't want to struggle and clash and not understand the person I was with. I wanted things to flow and for us to have a smoother path. The man I am with now is very different from me, but we complement each other very well. Out of all the relationships I have been in, this by far has been the easiest, the most compatible, and the most fun. Instead of fighting an uphill battle where we don't understand each other, we are almost always on the same side from the beginning. The arguments we have are few. The unmet needs are nearly non-existent, and I honestly do believe this is due to the fact that we are very compatible on paper.

Is this the be-all and end-all metric or barometer of relationships? Are you doomed if the one you choose doesn't fit your sign or your type on paper? No. If two people are committed to making anything work, it will work. Does this make things easier? I would say yes. Relationships are hard enough in this world we live in that is so full of distractions and division. Anything that makes the process easier is worth considering. Even if your dating profile offends men enough to call you batshit crazy because they are a Capricorn.

The Big Takeaway Question: What measures of compatibility are you willing to try?

I know this sounds crazy, but it really was the key to finding someone I was naturally compatible with. If you do not know what your love language is, research it so you can teach someone how to love you well.

THE LIST

Who you choose to spend your life with is the biggest decision you will ever make and can leave you either happy and content or stressed out and miserable. The ink wasn't dry on my divorce before I created the list. After nearly twenty years with the wrong guy, I was really specific about the qualities that I was looking for in my next partner. Being a really annoying list maker and goal setter, I put pen to paper one coffee-fueled morning and came up with my list of "must haves."

Happy
Positive outlook
Smart, gets my jokes and humor
Affectionate
Easy to be with
Has lots of friends
Has a warm accepting family
Plans adventures for us
Makes a great living

Hardworking, has a solid job and makes good decisions financially

Has no debt

Loves to travel

Accepts me as I am

Willing to talk about the hard things, a communicator

Supports my career

Loves my kids

Is an incredible father/step-father

Is patient and kind

Is calm in the face of drama

Is generous

Loves to surprise and spoil me

Has no addictions

Healthy physically, not a fanatic but maintains an active lifestyle

Easygoing and loves life

Has integrity

Honest and tells the truth, even when it's hard

Trustworthy, has never cheated

Amazing sexual chemistry, similar wants, frequency, and needs

Funny, lots of inside jokes

Likes to do things, especially new things

Extrovert

Has enormous penis

Is easy to be with, even if we are just staying at home

Is my best friend

Okay, okay, the penis thing I just threw in there to make sure you were still reading, but my point is a list like this is so helpful. Remember in your twenties, when your only relationship criteria was, "Is he hot?" Physical attraction was most of the reason you went out with someone. It wasn't based on anything real. It came down to, "Do I want to rip his clothes off? Yes. Then he's the one." As you age (Gawd, I sound a million years old with those three words), different things become important. You consider every aspect of them. Making sure you line up on things like finances and sex type and frequency, two of the biggest divorce reasons out there, suddenly becomes so much more important.

When you've had bad relationships, you can reverse engineer it and finally know what you do want in your partner. When you take the time to make a list like this, it solidifies your wants. People do this all the time when they are hunting for real estate. Your agent will always ask about your must-haves. Why don't you adopt this concept and design your perfect partner? Really, thoughtfully consider all aspects of what you are looking for, commit them to memory, and write them down. I have learned in life that writing things down is a powerful exercise because it gives your brain something concrete to focus on as you are out in the world, shifting and sorting through the available options out there.

I get a lot of shit for my list-making, but I will tell you this: the relationship I am in now with the right guy is incredible because he has almost all of these qualities. When we started dating, I even told him about my list, and he laughed and said, "You better send it over and let me see if I check all the boxes." I was too shy initially to do that and honestly didn't want him to see all my cards because it might have influenced him to present himself in a manner that wasn't authentic just to try to make me happy. As we spent more time together, I was able to evaluate that he was nearly exactly the dream guy I had ordered up when I wrote the list in the first place.

If you have never tried this exercise or think it's dumb, I invite you to push past those feelings and give it a shot. It can't hurt, right? And if it works, then you will have attracted your dream guy and life will be so much easier with him.

The Big Takeaway Question: What qualities does your ideal partner have?

Get specific. Anything that is important, even if it is small, is worth writing down. Knowing what you want makes it so much easier to find what you are looking for. You can do it in two ways. One way is to list characteristics you want in your partner, and the other is reverse engineering, knowing the qualities you know you absolutely cannot stand.

LET'S TALK ABOUT SEX, BABY

Sex is the hottest of the hot topics in relationships and for good reason, when it's good, it's mind-blowing and deeply connecting. In order for it to be good, you have to lay a foundation of love and respect. This takes time to develop and why I advocate waiting to be intimate until you are in a committed relationship. During the dating and discovery phase, becoming intimate too early can ruin something that has a chance at being real. It puts too much pressure on the early stages of the developing relationship. It's a bell you can't unring, and to be honest, sex too early is usually deeply unsatisfying because you don't know each other well enough yet.

Sex should be a shared physical and emotional experience, not a lever used to control or manipulate. It's about giving and accepting pleasure, never exchanging acts for favors, a change in relationship status, or worse material things. It's not a way to prove your worth or value to another human being. In its purest sense, inside a relationship, it's a declaration of love and mutual give and take. Outside of a committed relationship, it's reduced to a release. A release can be good, but you can muddy the waters significantly in the early stages of a real relationship if you rush into a physical one without taking the time to establish the foundation.

Physical touch is my number one love language, so physical chemistry with a partner was very high on my compatibility wish list. I also know that sex is very emotionally connecting for me, and in the past, if the relationship did not progress enough to be able to handle this, it crashed and burned under the weight of that need. I learned the hard way that by waiting, it gives the rest of the facets of the relationship a chance to catch up and eliminates that lopsided place you can land when you have sex too early.

Everyone has a different set of needs when it comes to sex. Some are once a week-ers, some are once a day-ers, some are kinky, some are vanilla. There's a big wide world of people out there who like all kinds of things, all kinds of ways. Personally, I am firmly in the camp of, if it is safe, sane, and consensual, then have a good time.

I am a big advocate for talking about it frequently, being upfront and honest, and to really narrow down your wants and needs to see if they match up with the person you are dating. You will save yourself so much pain and sorrow by lining up this critical metric with a person who can give to you the way you want it as often as you want it. Whatever your sexual orientation is, if you are asexual, you will find it easier to find an asexual partner to share your life with. There is no shame in what you want, how you want it, or even if you never want it.

Sex can either be an amazing time spent between two people or the biggest roadblock in your relationship. The most important key is finding someone whose wants and needs overlap closely with your own. If you have a deficit, that is going to become a problem. Maybe not today, but definitely sometime in the future, one of you will want a back rub that doesn't lead to sex, and the other one will be stuck in their own head feeling unwanted. It is a huge obstacle to overcome. The imbalance is the issue. You will eliminate dissatisfaction if you have the same basic wants in regard to frequency and style. Irritation sets in when there is a major discrepancy between partners. The frustration of not getting your sexual needs met will lead you to wander to places that make the relationship vulnerable to nearly anything.

Sex is a need, a drive that most people have that can't be stifled. It will eventually find its release. A person who is repeatedly denied will often resort to looking outside the relationship to get the need met. The need drives you to do things you wouldn't normally consider. Only after the need has been satisfied can you see the consequences, and by then, the damage has already been done.

Some people don't have the driving need for sex, and that is okay, too. In order to be in a satisfying, peaceful relationship you want to find someone who is compatible with you in the sex department, where your desires, frequency, and turn-ons align. If you use sexual compatibility as one of the determining criteria when you choose a partner, that will ensure you are on the same page and not allow resentment to build. Resentment in all its forms is detrimental to healthy relationships.

Sex dies in relationships that have no respect. If you let it die, it may feel incredibly hard to get that back. It will be work to rekindle the spark. If enough damage has been done, the fire might be out completely. That is another death. That is a relationship that is over. I hate to tell you there is no hope, but the mountain of work to come back from that is almost impossible to climb. You might think you hate sex, and then you find the right partner and are gobsmacked by how much you love it.

There is no greater connection you can have than an emotional and physical one combined, when you get to lose control in life and enjoy the pleasure of the person you love. There is nothing dirty or wrong about that. Inhibitions get in the way of that.

It's easy to look at your body and only see the imperfections, to only see the stretch marks and the extra bit of weight around your tummy or thighs. Women are especially good at this. Stop any woman on the street and ask her what she doesn't like about herself, and I bet she can instantly hit you with ten physical attributes she hates. Ask her what she likes about herself, and most women will struggle with this. That is sad and needs to change.

I can guarantee that most men don't spend a second focused on the imperfections you see. If you are excited and willing, that trumps everything. Men want to be with a woman who can relax enough to enjoy sex. Men especially like a woman who doesn't expect him to initiate all the time, a woman who shows her man that she wants him with words or a simple grab. I have initiated with a single word successfully, "Wanna?" It is truly that easy, and your man will LOVE that you want to be with him. Even inside a relationship, men fear rejection, so initiating is a way to even the effort, alleviate his fear, and he will appreciate it.

Let go. Let go of what is holding you back. To get to those world-shattering orgasms, you have got to get out of your own head. It is sexy as hell. There are not many times in this life that you get to be free. You owe it to yourself to figure out what you like. Yes, that means figuring out your body if you don't know how it works. Orgasms are good for your health, your sleep, and your fulfillment as a woman. When I hear that someone has never had one, it makes me sad. It is one of the greatest joys of life.

Sex flourishes in honest relationships. If you feel shame

or have debilitating inhibitions, you need to work to heal these parts of yourself. Sex is not dirty or wrong or immoral. If you like it rough or tender and sweet, it is your decision. You should be able to tell your partner your fantasies. If you can't speak openly about what turns you on, then you are in the wrong relationship. I hate to make it so simple, but I know this to be true.

Sex requires trust and vulnerability. When you come together sexually in a healthy relationship, it will be like everything is brand new. You will soar to higher highs than you ever have. It will be another incredible box you get to tick things off of that works in your relationship. You should be free to experience the highest expression of pleasure.

The Big Takeaway Question: What do you need to be satisfied sexually?

This is important. If you don't know this about yourself, start now and discover it. Having honest discussions with your partner about your wants, needs, and fantasies will give you a chance to discover if you are aligned. Compatibility about sex will make everything easier. If there is a vast discrepancy between what you want and what he wants, that is not the right guy.

IT'S JUST MONEY, HONEY!

I've had some, and I've had none. Money is a magnifier. If you are awesome, it makes you incredibly awesome, but if you are an asshole, it makes you a giant asshole. Money is a magical tool, and one of our best friends likes to call it fun coupons. That is the best way to look at something as polarizing as money. Money is another hot button issue that is the reason for many major headaches in relationships.

The best advice I was ever given was to look at finances as a game with your partner. You are on the same team, working toward the same goal. Your current financial situation is not the big deal breaker you think it is because, honestly, with the exception of an inheritance or trust fund, it can come and go. You can be flying high with your dream job one minute, and the next a pandemic can hit and you are reduced to being a lunch lady. Life turns on a dime. It has been especially crazy lately. There is no longer the push to go to college, to get a good job at a good company, and then work there for forty years and retire with a big, fat pension. We haven't been living in that world since 1989. Things move fast and furious. Jobs come and go, life changes quickly, and you need to pick someone who is on your side and who works to build your finances together, not undermines you every step of the way.

Money is a source of tension, especially since spenders and savers seem to be attracted to each other. I've been with men who are terrible with money and those who are responsible. For me, the responsible guy is the right call. My anxiety and stress levels are off the charts with someone who overspends, mostly because I have worked my whole life and greatly sacrificed not to be in debt. The resentment that builds up between partners who don't see eye to eye on finances is a major headache that I want to avoid at all costs.

If you want things to be easy, you should align on basic money principles. If you are a saver, it is easiest for you to match with another saver. If you're a spender, then someone who doesn't white-knuckle his credit card will be an easier fit and make for much more general happiness, though you will both need to learn to set healthy limits to keep you out of bankruptcy. You have to be a team. It will be less of a source of tension in your relationship if you line up on financial values.

Do not make the mistake of letting someone else make all the money decisions in your marriage or committed cohabitation situation. These are decisions that should be made together. If you are in a relationship and you don't know where your money goes, or what is in your accounts, this is unhealthy. Even if you hate learning about money, it is unhealthy to go through life unaware and irresponsible. Push yourself out of your comfort zone to learn about it. If you are in a relationship, and he controls the money and refuses to talk to you about it, that is dangerous territory and bordering on abuse. Money between partners should be something that is discussed frequently, and all big decisions should be decided on together. Cars, houses, vacations, and retirement goals should be mutual decisions.

If you are dating, looking for someone to take care of you financially sets up a power imbalance that will never work long-term. Marrying someone for money puts you in a weak state. You should never use it as a qualifier to decide if a partner is right for you. Do not look for someone to take care of you. You should be in a place where you can take care of yourself. Putting the burden of financial need on your partner will destroy any chance you have at a healthy relationship. You will be together because you need to be, not because you want to be.

There may be a disconnect between what you make and what your partner makes, but it is the effort that you are both putting in to make this part of your life flow. Over the course of many decades together, things can change drastically. Always viewing this area of your life as a partnership will help. No one person is fully responsible, and the burden is spread over the shoulders of two with the same shared mission.

Being financially responsible is something you can strive toward, no matter who you are with right now. It is a choice to align with behaviors that support the life you want to live. Shopping can become another survival buffering technique that can cause damage in your relationship, or personal strife if you are single. By learning how to manage your money in a healthy way, and by working together to build the life you want to live, you will remove this relationship stressor for good.

The Big Takeaway Question: How can you become financially responsible and take care of yourself?

You can do it. This will take so much pressure off your relationship and keep the dynamic healthy. If you are in a relationship, have those hard conversations about money. Listen for clues that tell you what he values or how he handles his financial affairs.

KIDS: THE CUTEST BAGGAGE OUT THERE

Dating is different when you have kids. Depending on their ages, it is something that you might have to consider this time around. You might have less time for dating in general because you are a soccer mom, or you might be head over heels with someone who doesn't like or want children. Your children must be considered carefully.

If they are under the age of ten, be very careful and watchful in the early stages. Never, ever leave them unattended with a new partner. I hate to throw out generalizations, but there are bad people that prey on single moms, knowing their resources are stretched thinner, knowing their bars are typically lower because they know they come with baggage.

Kids need stability and sameness, especially ones who have survived the trauma of divorce. Introducing them to men that aren't sticking around is a very bad idea because they also get attached. This is a very important time in their personal development. From toddlers to teenagers, you are writing on the slate of who they are. Every decision you make, and every person that is brought into their life, is being cataloged on their psyche. Even if they say nothing, they record it all and lock it away.

It will shape how they date, who they date, who they marry, and what their relationships look like forever. I am not exaggerating. They will have so many feelings regarding everything. They can feel like they are being replaced, they can be afraid of losing their time with you, and they can have anxiety in a blended family situation. They might not know anymore what their role is in your life. Change is very hard for kids to accept. Everyone will tell you that kids are resilient, and to a degree, that is true, but to me, resilience means they can survive a painful event like a divorce. I don't know about you, but as a mother, I want my kids to thrive, not just survive. Part of helping them thrive is protecting them from extraneous people that are temporary. Don't let them have the opportunity to become attached if you aren't rock-solid about the future of the relationship.

Never hide the fact that you have kids. Listen to the men you date, to the things they say about their own kids. Or, if they don't have any, what do they have to say about kids in general? Whatever his views are, he will not change. You cannot convince him otherwise. With my forever guy, the very last hoop he had to jump through was about my kids. I wanted to be with someone who enjoys my kids, who makes an effort to see them as people, and who has an open heart where they are concerned. We talked about it at length. He eventually met my daughter who is living with me, and over the course of the last two years, they have become allies united in their desire to make fun of me nearly constantly.

He researches her electronics purchases and floats her zero-interest loans to buy them that I never would. He talks to her about credit cards and listens to her terrible music because they have some overlapping tastes when he takes her for driving lessons. He makes an effort. That is all I really wanted, a man who makes a real effort to connect with my kids. Someone who understands how important they are in my life and who works to establish his own relationships with them.

The right guy will want to do this. He will put in the effort to create real relationships with them because he knows it is essential to your happiness. There are men out there who have space in their hearts for your children, and it is a beautiful thing to see a man choose to love a child that is not biologically his.

Maybe you don't have kids, but want them in the future. This is a very deep need, and you need to align with a healthy man on the same track with the same desire to be a parent. Or maybe a man you want to date has kids, and you are not interested in being a parent at all. Like it or not, he is a parent, and you will have to accept that and also accept the fact that the current custody arrangement might change. Even if he doesn't see them much now, life could change and he could be granted full custody. Are you willing to be a full-time stepmother if that should occur?

Wherever children are concerned, you both have to be brutally honest and accept the other person's decisions as absolute. Take time to examine your wants and needs where children are concerned and find a partner who aligns with you.

The Big Takeaway Question: What are your wants and needs in terms of parenting, co-parenting, and children? What role do you want your partner to play in these categories?

This is a big one and is the source of many conflicts in relationships. You must thoroughly examine where you are in your life and what you want in your life in regard to parenting and children, and so must your partner. In a serious relationship, you must align in this area, or the relationship will be very difficult to make successful.

THE VENN DIAGRAM OF US

Remember in the nineties when Jerry Maguire told us, "You complete me?" What a crock of shit that turned out to be. As a survivor of that movie, I found myself out there in my twenties, looking for my other half, someone to complete me, a failed errand if ever there was one.

Now, I see that it is more like a Venn Diagram. You are a complete circle, and your man is his own complete circle, and then there is the overlap of us. Keep in mind that life will be so much easier if your circle and your partner's circle have a lot of natural overlap. Not complete overlap, because variety keeps things interesting, but on many things, you agree. Mutual hobbies and values, when they overlap, will naturally make the bumpy process of coupling up that much smoother.

Your mission is to own your circle. Figure yourself out fully, what you love and what you hate. Find the things that light you up inside and make your life interesting. Go out and fill your circle with as much fun and flair in whatever flavor it comes in for you, confident in the knowledge that, by knowing yourself this way and being complete on your own, you will attract a man whose diagram will overlap yours. Don't be coy or wishy-washy. Own your crazy. Own who you are and what you are passionate about. It is the only way to put out the bat signal for the relationship you are looking for. Don't make concessions. Be unapologetically you.

Complete *yourself*. Take as much time as you need to do this because, if you don't, one way or another, life will demand you to do it by forcing you with painful circumstances. The work waits. It might be a little niggling in the back of your mind. It might be an all at once total destruction that sets you on this path. Either way, it is time to complete your circle. Fill that baby up with your favorite things. Cram that circle with the life you want to live and the experiences you still want to enjoy.

If you are in your twenties, be smarter than I was, and take the time to figure yourself out while you are young. This way, you won't be forced to do it in your forties and in front of the captive audience of your children. It's much easier to undertake this work without those distractions. I was a slow learner. I didn't really do the work of completing myself until I was over forty and had teenagers. I give that experience a one star. Do not recommend. It's like trying stand-up comedy for the first time and having a heckler destroy you on stage. A heckler that you created yourself.

If I had done the work on myself early on, my life would have been drastically different. It is one of my greatest regrets in life. Jumping into the next relationship and then the next one without this critical time of self-discovery definitely hindered my progress.

So, take the advice of an old lady. Complete yourself. Now. It's that important.

The Big Takeaway Question: What do you need to complete your circle?

Complete yourself, darling. It is what you were born to do. Do not put that task in someone else's hands. They won't even begin to know how to do it. No matter where you are or how much time has passed, start right now. Complete yourself.

IT'S IMPOSSIBLE TO FUCK UP THE RIGHT THING

It is truly impossible to fuck up the right thing. Commit this to memory. Make it into a mantra you repeat over and over to yourself until it sticks. This will set you free. When you finally meet someone who has possibility, who could be a contender, you end up scaring them away by spreading your anxiety all over them. You coat them in it, talking them out of liking you, or maybe even loving you because your mind searches for problems. It wants to protect you, so it is constantly scanning the field for problems, for errors that could signal this isn't going to work. It will start clanging the warning bell before you even give things a chance, prematurely ending something that had the possibility of being great. The fear will send you to the corner to lick your wounds again, soothing yourself with the small victory of, "Hey, at least I didn't put it all out there."

When it is right, you cannot fuck it up. You cannot push away the heart that is meant to love you. You can't. Yes, you can and will make mistakes, but the heart that is yours will accept the apology. It will give you the benefit of the doubt when you don't deserve it. It will give you a free pass when you're a crazy bitch.

The right person can see you at your worst, when you are covered in hormonal acne and eating cookie dough right out of the tube, and he will love you anyway. The wrong person can see you at your very best and at your highest high and cut you down and make you feel insignificant.

The fear of losing something awesome is a real fear. I get that. I felt it, too. After years of terrible choices in relationships, I finally attracted a healthy human. But almost immediately after the sweet, swoony, dopamine inspired feelings of love hit my brain, they were replaced by the fear of losing this unicorn. A brain that is used to fear will always go back to it. Fear is all it knows. It feels normal, it is ingrained, and it is a repetitive pattern that you have played out over and over again. The fear will scream, "You will never find another man like this! Hold on tight!" This is where the settling and hiding become the crutch you lean on too heavily to protect yourself, but ends up just slowing down the inevitable.

Clinging to a relationship in fear is a powerless place to be. It weakens everything. It colors every interaction in stress and suspicion. It chases away the happiness and sweetness because both of these states can't simultaneously exist. It makes you do dumb things, like stalk your boyfriend on social media and look at his phone when he's in the shower, surveilling everything and gathering supporting evidence like you are on a hunt to expose him and say, "Ah-ha! I knew it. I knew this was too good to be true." What kind of relationship can withstand that kind of scrutiny?

What if there was a better way? What if you could relax into knowing that, if it's the right thing, everything will work out? If it's the right relationship, you will be able to overcome huge obstacles and still find a way to love and support the other person? What if you just decided to let go of the fear for once? Just let go of the worry and instead tuned in to bringing the best part of yourself to every interaction with them, so you could see more accurately if this was the right relationship? And, so what if it turns out that it wasn't? Instead of holding on tight to a sack full of crap, languishing for years and wasting your time, you could drop it and walk away. Knowing it wasn't yours. No hesitation, none of this, "No one is perfect, but he's good enough," nonsense. You could make a decision and move forward instead of being paralyzed by fear and staying stuck in the wrong thing for years.

When you hide who you are in an attempt to influence others to like you, they don't get to see the real you. They see the fake you that you have allowed them to see. Then, about six months in, when you are tired of being the fake you, the gloves come off and you let more authentic pieces of yourself dribble out. It's a bait and switch that really serves no one. When you can be unapologetically who you are, and comfortable enough to be that vision of yourself with your partner, then you are free. Then you are building something that will last. It's efficient, it is honest, and it is a great use of your time.

Your desperate clinging to something that is only partially right does nothing but slow the process down to a standstill. You must have a willingness to see that everything you go through in life builds you up instead of tearing you down. Over time, the plan makes sense, but seeing it in the moment will make you doubt the process. It's like when contractors tear down old houses with beach views. The new house they construct in its place is always far more beautiful. But on the journey to better, there is always a fair amount of destruction before the construction can take place.

When you can quickly let go of the wrong thing, you open a space for the right thing to come. When you can look at your relationships honestly and through the lens of truth, you can make decisions about the future there. It is not muddled with the emotions of worry and anxiety and settling. It is crystal clear and easy to read. It is fresh and simple.

It is truly impossible to fuck up the right thing, and incredibly easy to fuck up the wrong one. So, let go of the fear and embrace this permission to be unapologetically you. The faster you do this, the faster you will align with the right person.

The Big Takeaway Question: Are you afraid you will fuck it up?

Journal on the fears you feel until you find the root. Often times, these fears are from childhood where you didn't feel loved by a parent, or didn't feel like anything you did was good enough. These are the things you need to heal. Acknowledging them first, forgiving, and letting go are part of the healing process. You are enough. You are worthy of an incredible relationship that fits the greatest parts of you, and when you find it, you will not fuck it up. Because you can't.

HE IS NOT YOUR EVERYTHING

I love a mushy, gooey love proclamation like everyone else. Romantic and sweet declarations make me weak in the knees. Except for one. "He is my everything." He is not your everything. If he is, there is an imbalance that needs to be corrected. It is dangerous and unhealthy to give your power away like that. If he is truly your everything, then what happens if things don't work out, or he dies, or he cheats on you?

If he truly is your everything, then you cease to exist. Having a healthy relationship with the right person is many things. He can be your best friend, your favorite person, your partner in crime. He can be your co-pilot, your rock, your soft place to fall. But never give someone else everything. Give him your excess. He is your extra, your bonus points, your cherry on the top of your sundae.

Think about the pressure you are putting on him. The stakes are so much higher when someone is your everything. Instead of approaching the relationship lighthearted and easy, it is steeped in obligation and responsibility for someone else's happiness. I'm not sure which is worse, putting your happiness in someone else's hands or having someone else's happiness depend on you. Both are equally heavy and hard, and the weight of them will crack even the strongest relationships. Relationships function better and grow when each person is responsible for themselves. When each half is self-aware enough to understand that making yourself happy is the key. When each person shows up with the best and healthiest mindset they can have, not needing anything from the other to feel better, but able to draw from their own resources.

The Big Takeaway Question: Who is your everything?

I'll give you a hint. You look at her every morning when you brush your teeth.

YOU'VE MADE IT TO THE FINAL QUESTION

The final question is the biggest one with the farthest-reaching consequences.

What do you really want?

For the most part, I think society is just full of the walking dead. Zombies, getting up, going to work, going to college, having kids, eating, sleeping, and pooping on autopilot. No one is feeling anything anymore, and when they do, enter alcohol or drugs or eating or shopping or any other addiction that will distract you back into the calm place where you don't have to think and you get to live your zombie lifestyle again.

At any point, you can turn this bus around and make a different decision that can lead you to a completely different life. If you are unhappy, change something. Don't let days, months, or years tick by feeling stuck, unsatisfied, and off course. Take the responsibility for bringing joy into your own life. Let go of what has been holding you back, forgive those you need to forgive, and move on.

Hold on loosely and walk through life with an open heart. Stop apologizing, and stop holding on to the things that don't serve you. Stop punishing yourself and holding onto the past.

Step into your new future, lighter, freed from the burdens of shame and doubt. I hope you work through the takeaway questions and dig deep. I hope that, somehow, I have rearranged the twenty-six letters of the alphabet in this book in such a way that it changes your life. My greatest wish is that something I have said here sticks and inspires you to undergo your own personal transformation. If you have only completed the first part, then I am so truly happy to have been part of this journey to reclaim yourself.

If you have taken it a step further and found someone to share your overflow with, then I am thrilled for you because life is infinitely more fun when you have someone to share it with. But completing this part is not a requirement to have a happy fulfilling life.

The insights you have learned through this journey will benefit every relationship in your life. Most importantly, it will impact the relationship you have with yourself. The new skills you have acquired will help you build better friendships and be a better parent. When put into practice daily, all the relationships in your life will improve.

Thank you for reading this book. It has truly been a labor of love for me, and I can't wait to hear the ways your life begins to change when you start showing up for yourself. Let me know on social media, or join my Facebook exclusive reader group, the Ninyons. We have a lot of fun in there, and I promise I will make you laugh once or twice.

No matter what, you are loved, you deserve a beautiful life that fulfills you in every way, and you are the only one who can bring that dream life into reality. You are worth it. Now go get it!

XOXO Ninya

ACKNOWLEDGMENTS

I have to thank Brooke. Fate brought her into my life over the course of the last year, and she has pushed me to carefully think about my writing in ways that I have never been pushed before. To have a champion hold a mirror to you when you are screwing up and say, "You can do better," or a cheerleader clapping the loudest when you hit the finish line on important work is a gift. Brooke pushes me to work harder and dive deeper. My writing is stronger because she is unafraid to tell me the truth. I adore her honesty and authenticity and the time she has given to me so freely when I have been unable to repay her. I hope everyone reading this book has a Brooke in their lives. The older I get, the more I cherish fierce lady friendships that are built on trust, honesty, and vulnerability. I love you, Brooke.

And to Kendra, my amazing editor, who works so hard to make me look literate. After a year together, I trust you implicitly. I value your feedback and friendship, and you are part of my tribe, even if you do eat candy corn. You are a diamond.

CHECK OUT MY MEMOIR, SCOTLAND WITH A STRANGER

Who goes to Scotland for two weeks with a stranger they met over the internet?

I did.

I remember the very first message; I was part of a women's photography group on Facebook, and I was nearing the end of my photography career. It was an uncertain time, and I was trying to figure out what was next for me professionally. This coated my life in fear that was nearly paralyzing, like a boat floating in the ocean, no longer tethered to the career that had been my identity. The last three years after my divorce had been punishing in nearly every measurable way, and I was completely depleted.

At the time, I was working exclusively from home, rarely leaving the house because, when I am depressed, I tend to hunker down and hide. I was sad and lost, and nothing seemed to make sense anymore, stuck in the soul sucking social media career I never wanted but which seemed to want me. The daily grind of it and the comparison factor left the sour taste of dissatisfaction in my mouth when I looked at the smoking wreckage of my life. Social media is the devil, camouflaged as connection. Showing us the greatest hits reels of people's lives, which we compare against our personal struggles, making us feel insignificant, unworthy, and less than. I was stuck in this land of fraud and make believe, unable to find an exit.

Every day was the same, stretched out before me, looking bleak and barren, and I just existed in the most basic ways, only fulfilling the basic needs for myself and my children. That day, I posted a photo in the group of the five-figure engagement ring I had just returned to the wrong man, needing some encouragement from strangers because my life was so isolating. And then I heard the Facebook messenger notification *ding*, and there it was. A message from a stranger named Erika.

> I read your post. I have this idea I want to do. I know the mountains of Scotland. When I had to take my life back, I took off for Scotland and hiked and hiked and found myself again on the mountains. It was amazing.
>
> I want to take a group of women there. Not like a workshop. But more just for self-healing. There is something special about Scotland. And don't worry, I know how to do it cheap.
>
> I pray a lot, and when I was there last time, I knew I was supposed to do this.
>
> I will just lead you. When I was there last time, I knew this was something I was called to do. I know the country. I know what you are going through, and I know the need to regain your sense of self. This is a God thing.

A God thing. The magic words. It hit my heart hard. I was raised Catholic, and it stuck, especially the guilt. I didn't identify as Catholic anymore, but I definitely believed in God, and nothing would ever change that. I have always had a wide-eyed optimistic 'Pollyanna' quality, always thinking things will get better, even when knee deep in disaster. I should have been a boxer. My ability to recover, knockout after knockout, was so strong, like one of those weighted superhero punching bags that take a pounding and then pop right back up again, over and over and over.

Hiking, healing, the trip of a lifetime... These words resonated in the deepest recesses of my heart. Being a self-help junkie since nearly birth, my library was filled with inspirational books, my favorites being those of journey and self-discovery stories like *"Wild"* and *"Eat Pray Love."* Those stories planted a seed in me that yearned for an experience like this, and the idea that I might *actually* have one in real life was thrilling.

It called to my soul in a way that there was nothing else I could say except yes. It just felt like it was the exact thing I needed, at the exact, right moment I needed it.

The messages flew back and forth furiously for a few minutes. Erika would plan everything. I would just need to show up and be transformed.

> **The people there are so happy.**
> **Happiness and joy like you have never experienced before.**
> **The landscape is so beautiful.**
> **The mountains and waterfalls are amazing.**
> **When I got to the summit, I cried.**

Beauty. Joy. Happiness. I could use some of that. Those things had been so elusive for me for so long, I almost forgot they existed. She said we could do it all for less than $3000, so I made up my mind in seconds. I had been dying to use my passport since I got it a year and a half before. I had never been out of the country, ever, not even to Canada or Mexico, and I was ready! I was finally going to travel and do all the things I said I was going to do 'someday.' I was going to heal myself and reconnect with my soul on the mountaintops of Scotland. Finally, I was going to fill up my own well and figure out who I was now that I had no man in my life.

When I read her words through my cracked rose-colored glasses, I sobbed like a baby at the rightness of it all. When the student is ready, the teacher appears. I could not have been more excited and ready for an experience like this.

The next day, I wrote in my journal:

God sent me an angel in Erika. A guide, a leader, a sister. Someone who has been there. Who knows the struggle to get back to your sense of self when you have lost everything. When you don't know who you are anymore. When you are little and lost and broken. Someone who can gently guide you back to center. Who can push you to break through the sadness and pain to the other side. That is what Erika will do for me. I just know it.

Fair warning: I must also admit I have a flair for the dramatic and over romancing things in my head. Looking back now, I was a sitting duck. I mean, "God sent me an angel?" "When the student is ready, the teacher appears?" "Reconnect with my soul on the mountaintops of Scotland?" Reading those words now makes me want to puke in my mouth a little, but at the time, I was serious. It felt *so* right. It was *destiny*.

Yes, I am in. I am *all* in.

I needed this so badly.

That's how it started. A Facebook post in a group and a message from a stranger. That's all it takes to change your life.

CLICK HERE TO ORDER SCOTLAND WITH A STRANGER

ALSO BY NINYA

Velvet Guild Collection 1 Episodes 1-4

Velvet Guild Collection 2 Episodes 5-8

Velvet Guild Collection 3 Episodes 9-12

Velvet Guild Collection 4 Episodes 13-16

Scotland with a Stranger: A Memoir

First You Then Him: A Former Trainwreck's Guide to Becoming and then Finding a Healthy Partner

Buy direct from the author and Save 20% at checkout with code SAVE20

https://shop.ninya.us/collections/books-by-ninya

ABOUT THE AUTHOR

After nearly 40 years of denying who I am and what I was put here to do, I have finally claimed my place in the world. I am a writer. Better late than never, am I right?

I am working on a BDSM serial right now, "Velvet Guild." Each episode is approximately 65 pages/13,000 words and can be read in an hour, like an episode of Netflix. "Scotland with a Stranger: A Memoir" published June 2020.

I live near Des Moines, Iowa with an incredibly artistic and brilliant 15 year old who mocks me daily for my lack of style and who can draw on their eyebrows with the confidence of a drag queen.

Visit me online: https://ninya.us/
On Facebook:

www.ingramcontent.com/pod-product-compliance
Lightning Source LLC
Chambersburg PA
CBHW031057080526
44587CB00011B/725